Financial Aspects of Supervisory Management

Financial Aspects of Supervisory Management

J. E. SMITH BSc, FCWA, J.Dip.MA, MBIM

Senior Lecturer
Department of Industrial Administration
University of Aston in Birmingham

G. H. RAY BCom FCA

Lecturer
School of Management
University of Bath

NELSON

Thomas Nelson and Sons Ltd
Nelson House Mayfield Road
Walton-on-Thames Surrey KT12 5PL
P.O. Box 18123 Nairobi Kenya
Watson Estate Block A 13 Floor
Watson Road Causeway Bay Hong Kong
116-D JTC Factory Building
Lorong 3 Geylang Square Singapore 14

Thomas Nelson Australia Pty Ltd
19–39 Jeffcott Street West Melbourne Victoria 3003

Thomas Nelson and Sons (Canada) Ltd
81 Curlew Drive Don Mills Ontario

Thomas Nelson (Nigeria) Ltd
8 Ilupeju Bypass PMB 21303 Ikeja Lagos

First published in Great Britain 1967
Reprinted 1969
First published in paperback edition 1973
Reprinted 1976, 1977, 1978, 1980

ISBN 0 17 741004 3
NCN 5691 41 4

Printed in Hong Kong

Preface

This book is intended to explain to supervisory managers how the financial aspects of business operations impinge upon their activities. Accounting is often called the language of business, and this book deals with the ways in which this language may be used in situations familiar to the supervisory manager. It contains material which has not only been extensively used with supervisors from many industries, but has also introduced undergraduates and postgraduates to the financial aspects of industrial management problems. While primarily written for students taking the Certificate in Supervisory Studies, it is also suitable for those taking the Institute of Supervisory Management examination, and should provide a good introduction for anyone taking a Diploma in Management.

In the first five chapters we deal with the general area of finance and financial accounting. We show how finance is attracted to a business, and must then be used effectively; we also indicate how financial statements are constructed, and how success may be measured. The approach used should allow a supervisory manager to read financial statements, and to recognize strengths and weaknesses in such statements—matters which need to be understood if proper judgments are to be made.

Chapters 6 to 11 are concerned with management accounting. Management itself involves planning, taking actions, and evaluating the results of these actions. We have tried to show how management accounting is an information service which should assist in the execution of these managerial activities. The accountant plays an essential role here, for he provides information which can be used to evaluate performance and assist in the solution of business problems, including a choice between alternative courses of action.

The final chapter outlines the important relationship which exists between industry and the state, emphasizing the functions of planning and controlling operations.

J. E. S.

G. H. R.

Contents

CHAPTER 1 | Capital and Profit

Capital is in use all around you. Whether you are a supervisor of a manufacturing department or a service department, a garage, a car repair unit, or a shop, it is there for you to use effectively or otherwise. What does it comprise?

Let us say that you run a machine shop. One would not dare hazard a guess as to the state of the buildings, but you have some around you. They cost money to buy, or to lease from the rightful owner. Those buildings stand on land, which again your organization has purchased or leased. If this has been purchased recently, then the cost has been considerable. In one very well-known industrial area in Great Britain, the land costs approximately £2 per square foot to buy at the present moment. Can you think of any other capital in use which is like the items of buildings and land already mentioned? Yes, plant and machinery and equipment of all sorts, your radial drilling machines and your planers, the overhead travelling crane, the fixtures and fittings in your departmental stores for tools and consumable items, the fork lift truck and its pallets.

Fixed Assets

Do these items mentioned so far have anything in common? You may have spotted that they are all relatively permanent items—permanent in the sense that you expect to have them with you for some time. They are not likely to be used up in one year. Or to put it another way, when they are purchased they are expected to have a life measured in years. We call these *fixed asset* or *permanent asset* items. They are assets, in the sense that they are properties belonging to the proprietors of the business.

Current Assets

But all of the capital in use around you is not of this type. What else is there? Materials come into your shop. We can think of the raw materials which come in to be processed and the components for machining. In addition, there are the tools and consumable items, the maintenance materials and spare parts which have to be used. As the supervisor of the department, you will have a labour force to manage, and this manpower is paid wages for its services. Some are paid for engaging in productive effort, that is, actually changing

1

the shape or conformation of the article, product, or component. Some are paid for carrying out what are often called the indirect or non-productive jobs, the labouring, cleaning and sweeping, movement and handling of materials and products, and maintenance of equipment.

There are many other expenses, also. Electricity is used for power to drive the machines and for lighting. You may use gas and other fuels, slurry and compressed-air services. The supervisor of the department has a shop office, gets paid a salary, and incurs cost of stationery and office requisites. We are now talking of another type of capital in use in the department. This is *working capital*, in that the costs are day-to-day recurring costs, which come up again and again. These costs are expended in production, and depend to some extent upon the throughput of the department. At any time they are vested in work-in-progress, and these assets we call *current assets*, because they are current or moving; they change from day to day. New jobs and production orders are started, and others are completed. These assets could not be called permanent or fixed.

Let us summarize. The capital in use in the department which you supervise is of these two types:

Fixed Assets	*Current Assets*
Land	Work-in-progress, into which has
Buildings	gone materials, labour, and many
Plant, machinery, and equipment	other items of expense
fixtures and fittings	

Of course, if we look at the business as a whole for a moment, then it will be apparent that the range of fixed and current assets is much wider than it is in the individual department. There are office and selling departments where we would find other fixed assets, such as office machinery and sales representatives' cars. There is the finished stock of the company's products—this is another current asset item like work-in-progress in the shop. The company has cash at the bank, and has customers who owe the company money— again these are current assets, changing from day to day. Cash at bank is constantly changing as customers pay, then bills have to be paid, and cheques have to be drawn to pay suppliers of raw materials (called creditors), and to pay wages. The amount owed by customers, or debtors, as they are called, is being added to as further goods are sent to them, and being diminished as they send cheques in payment of their accounts.

This structure of fixed and current assets applies all through every business and has certain implications.

Implications of Assets

Fixed assets are permanent. This means that when a decision has been taken about the purchase of such an item, it is a conscious decision to saddle the business with a burden for a long time. Such a decision should be taken with care. Purchase of a machine can mean a large sum of money, which will take many years to recoup, going out of the business on one day.

There is a major problem here for the company, to ensure that the fixed assets are used as fully and as effectively as possible. We have seen in our machine shop that the supervisor is working with many items of fixed assets. It follows that he has a responsibility to ensure that these are efficiently used.

Working capital has different implications. There is a movement to it, which is depicted in Fig. 1.

The implication of this chart of working capital is that cash is flowing out of the business up to and including the point where the customer, or debtor, takes delivery of the finished goods. When the customer pays, cash is flowing back, and if the goods are yielding a profit the working capital circle is getting bigger. The amount of working capital will be increasing all the time in a profitable company, subject to periodic withdrawals from it. These withdrawals will be:

(a) *Expenditure on fixed assets.* Such expenditure will take money from the working capital area and deposit it in the fixed asset area in the form of land, buildings, plant, and equipment. This has the effect of reducing the amount of current assets available for stocks, work-in-progress, and lying in the hands of debtors.

(b) *Tax payments made annually.* Profit is being made, on which Corporation Tax is levied. This will be paid from cash resources annually, and is money flowing out of the business.

(c) *Annual dividend payments.* If we are talking of a company where part of the capital has come from the issue of shares, then the shareholders will expect to get annual dividends. These, when paid, will be cash flowing out of the business.

(d) *Cash put into other investments.* It might be advisable, on occasion, to pull money out of the working capital area and invest it outside the business.

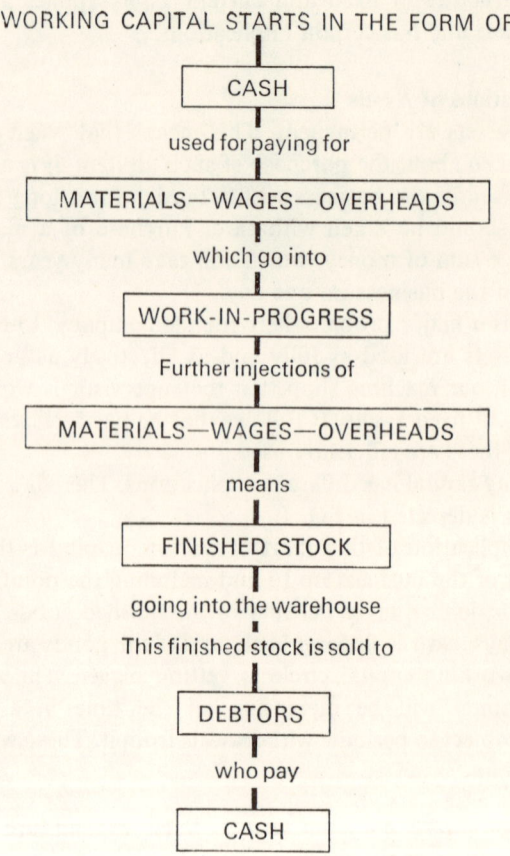

WORKING CAPITAL STARTS IN THE FORM OF

CASH

used for paying for

MATERIALS—WAGES—OVERHEADS

which go into

WORK-IN-PROGRESS

Further injections of

MATERIALS—WAGES—OVERHEADS

means

FINISHED STOCK

going into the warehouse
This finished stock is sold to

DEBTORS

who pay

CASH

FIG. 1. *Movement of working capital*

We now can see that speed of cash flow is crucial in a business—the assets must be kept moving. This is as much up to the supervisor or departmental manager, and under his control, as it is the responsibility of the accountant, the production controller, or the sales manager. Throughput in the supervisor's department is important to control of these cash flows: for example, an inordinately large amount of work-in-progress may well absorb much more of an organization's cash resources than it can afford. A supervisor may well have several thousand pounds of working capital on the move in his department at any time. This can be critical to the business.

Sources of Capital

Where does the capital come from? There are many sources from which a business may attempt to obtain the capital which it needs. Very much will depend upon how much capital is required, when it is required, whether the requirement is of short- or medium- or long-term nature, and many other factors, of which the cost of capital is one. In fact, capital is usually classified in the following manner:

A *Permanent or long-term*
   1 Share capital.
   2 Profits saved up, or retained earnings, as they are frequently called.
B *Medium-term*
   1 Loan capital generally.
   2 Debentures, in particular.
C *Short-term*
   1 Bank overdraft.
   2 Creditors, that is suppliers who are prepared to allow the business to purchase goods and services on credit.
   3 Special creditors, such as the Inland Revenue, to whom tax owed in the short term can be considered as additional capital.

We will examine these classes of capital in some detail shortly, but it may be as well to consider the factors which would guide the choice of the precise source of capital.

When a man starts a business on his own, we refer to him as a sole trader. In the first instance, he provides his own personal capital, and this is gradually added to by profits made which he does not draw out of the business. If, because of a likely or planned expansion of operations, this trader requires additional capital, he would presumably be happy to supply this capital himself, if he were in a position to do so. If he went to the bank to secure an overdraft, he would be required to pay interest at the rate of, say, 2% over the Bank Rate on the amount of the overdraft. Also, he would be required to pay back the loan within a short period, at a time not necessarily convenient to him. If he tries to secure the additional capital from another person, it would either be in the form of a loan, on which interest would again have to be paid, or the sole trading business would become a partnership, with implications as to the management and control of its operations.

The nature of the requirement would be very significant. It

could be that the additional capital required was needed permanently, as in the purchase of expensive fixed asset items, in which case additional personal capital would be the most logical solution. On the other hand, if the additional capital were required to support a rapid short-term expansion of production and sales quantities, then —providing such activities were profitable—the cash could be expected to flow back into the business fairly quickly. In this case, it would be more appropriate to look for short-term capital in the form of a short-term loan or a bank overdraft. Again, we are talking of cash flows. A big factor in deciding the most appropriate source of capital will be the nature of the cash inflows in the period following the use of the capital.

There is no fundamental difference when the sole trading business has become a partnership, or the partnership has become a limited company. A limited company's requirements for capital will vary, sometimes being for amounts to cover short-term expansion, sometimes being for larger amounts to cover spending on fixed assets. The directors of the company will need to take into account the possibility of spreading the net of shareholding, the cost of capital which can be afforded, bearing in mind the use to be made of the capital, and also current capital gearing. When we talk of capital gearing, we mean the relationship existing between the various sources of capital currently in use. For example, the capital subscribed by shareholders in the business may be £10,000, whereas the capital attracted from loan and overdraft sources may total £5,000. At this point we can refer to the latter type of capital as debt capital. Now, the permanent capital is currently twice the amount of the debt capital. If the business needs an injection of another £10,000 of capital, to what source should we go? Apart from all the other considerations mentioned, there is the important consideration of how shareholders would view more debt capital being required. Also, how will the suppliers of loans view the amount of debt capital becoming a bigger figure than the amount of permanent capital? This must now be seen as a significant factor.

Most supervisory managers will work for limited companies, so we will look at the capital structure of such companies.

Permanent or Long-term Capital
Share capital. A shareholder is a person who has subscribed capital to a business. In return he has received a share certificate detailing his holding in the company. It should be made clear that the implication of the phrase 'limited company' is that the share-

holders have a limited liability. That is, they cannot be called upon to accept responsibilities for the debts of a company for amounts over and above the issue price of their shares. There are several classes of shares, of which the most important is the Ordinary share.

The *Ordinary shareholders* provide the risk-bearing capital of a company, and normally carry voting rights which confer the ultimate control of the company upon them. Such risk-bearing deserves the greater proportion of the profits available for distribution, so that no fixed rate of dividend is accorded to ordinary shares. The dividend rate is declared annually and is dependent upon profits. Ordinary shareholders are often called equity shareholders, implying that they are entitled to the equity of the business—that is, the assets remaining after all other claims have been met.

Companies often issue *Preference shares,* which normally entitle the holders to receive a fixed percentage of dividend before any profits made are divided among other classes of shareholders. Such shareholders are often accorded preference in regard to repayment of capital in the event of winding up. Holders of such shares are not usually allowed to vote except in exceptional circumstances, as when dividends are in arrears, or in the event of winding up. Preference shares are often cumulative in type, which means that arrears of dividend are carried forward to be paid before dividends are declared on the risk-bearing Ordinary shares. Some companies issue Preference shares which are liable to be redeemed—that is, there is a stated future date at which such capital will be repaid to the holder In this way, what would normally be thought of as permanent capital can be rendered more short-term.

It is possible to issue non-voting Ordinary shares. This has often been done to retain control of the company in the hands of the original shareholders. A further justification for the issue of such shares is often said to be that the market for a company's shares will be widened. But this is often not so in practice, because the effect of such an issue is to create two classes of shares, one of which sells at a premium over the other. It can be argued that the issue of non-voting shares is undemocratic, and that holders of equity share capital should not be expected to take the risks involved without having opportunity to exercise control of the company.

There are also *Founders' shares,* which are sometimes issued to the original promoters of a company. They may be entitled to an agreed high rate of dividend and, at the same time, have the same voting rights as Ordinary shares.

Shares may be issued at a premium or at a discount. In the case

of shares issued at a premium, the share is issued at a price in excess
of its nominal or par value. In Great Britain, all shares have such a
nominal or par value, often £1, but the market price of shares varies
according to supply and demand for them. A company making a
new issue of, say, £1 shares, at a time when the market price was,
say, £2·50, would obviously want to make the issue price com-
mensurate with the market price. In this case, it would issue at
a premium of approximately £1·50 per share. The amount of the
premium would constitute additional capital for the company.
The issue of shares at a discount is rather more rare. Such an issue
must be given Court permission, and must be of a class of shares
already issued. In this case, for example, a share with a nominal
value of £1 might be issued for 95p, so reducing the actual money
capital intake. Normally, to put shares on the market at a discount
would be an admission that the company was in financial difficulties,
so that such issues are rarely contemplated.

Profit saved. A good way to raise capital is to make profit and
save it. An efficient company will make profits and will not distribute
all of them, but will use part of the increase in working capital for
the replacement of existing fixed assets or the acquisition of new
ones. This technique of retaining profit within the company is often
called ploughing back profits, and the capital so obtained could
be called internally generated capital. This procedure of using
internal capital resources is particularly appropriate to the smaller
company, since larger companies find it more easy to attract capital
from external sources.

Medium-term Capital

Loan capital generally. Capital can be acquired from loan
sources. In those instances where a company requires additional
capital, but where the requirement is of medium term only, it may be
obtained by borrowing money from various sources, such as a bank.
It is not conventional for banks to lend money for indefinite or long
periods of time, but they are willing to assist businesses, particularly
smaller ones, with loans specifically to enable them to purchase
additional capital asset items. The larger type of business might go
further afield, to financial institutions, to obtain loans. Predominant
among these are two established with Government approval, known
as the Finance Corporation for Industry Limited and the Industrial
and Commercial Finance Corporation Limited. The operations of
these organizations are intended to supplement the activities of
other lending institutions. The former concerns itself with amounts

of £200,000 and over, while the latter advances amounts from £5,000 up to £250,000. The intention of these bodies is also to bridge the gap which exists between short-term facilities on the one hand, and the long-term loans which may be gleaned from insurance companies and private finance houses on the other.

Debentures. A particular form of loan capital is the debenture. A debenture is a document issued by a company in acknowledgment of a debt, undertaking to pay interest on the amount of the debt, usually half-yearly, and to make repayment of the amount of the debt on or before a specified date. A debenture is either a 'simple' or 'naked' debenture or a 'mortgage' debenture.

In the case of a simple debenture, the loan is not secured in any way on the assets of the company. This means that, in the event of winding up, a debenture holder ranks with other unsecured creditors for repayment of debts, and has no prior claim. It is more usual for a debenture to be secured on the assets of the company, in which case it is referred to as a mortgage debenture. This security may be on a specific asset item, or on the assets generally.

Debentures are quite frequently issued at a discount and may be redeemable at a premium. There is no legal restriction to the issue of these documents at a discount. In fact, by exercising this particular right a company may be able to obtain the advantage of an issue at a lower rate of interest.

Short-term Capital

Bank overdraft. This is a very common method of raising short-term capital. A bank will normally offer this service to a business which is financially sound, but which has some temporary short-term difficulty with regard to working capital. It is common for some organizations to use overdraft facilities for very lengthy periods, but the interest charges are relatively expensive.

Creditors. Those organizations which supply a company with materials and services on credit are supplying capital. This is of a short-term type, in that their invoices have usually to be met on monthly account. Nevertheless, this is a very useful form of capital. When working capital is short, some companies will delay settlement of creditors' accounts, but in the longer term this practice could have damaging effects.

Special creditors. There are many of these. For example, any tax owed to the Inland Revenue in the short term can be regarded as additional capital until the payment is made. Assets can be purchased on hire purchase or instalment payment terms. It is possible to borrow money from discount houses on some security, such as the documents of title to goods.

In fact, there are other sources of capital also. The sale and lease-back of freehold land and buildings has been a popular method in recent years. Here the company sells a property at a price greatly in excess of its original capital cost and leases the property at an agreed lease rental for a specified period. Capital can in effect be obtained by leasing equipment rather than by making an outright purchase.

Using Capital

It should now be clear that there is capital in use in the business, and that it may have come from different sources. Remember that the capital costs money in the form of dividends or interest, and that the people who subscribe it have a right to see it intelligently, economically, and effectively used. What does this imply? It means that the supervisory manager, as a user of capital, has a responsibility to ensure that the assets of the business, both fixed and current, are effectively employed. Effective use of capital means capital put to profitable use. This is demonstrated in Fig. 2.

At the top of this chart we see the main sources of capital which have been outlined in this chapter. Capital is put to use—that is, it is spent on purchasing and providing the fixed assets and the current assets. These assets are all used to make goods, products, and services for sale. When we sell these commodities and services, we should make a profit on them. Whether we in fact make a profit or not depends upon our efficiency in making the product and selling it, the accuracy of our selling prices, the volume of business we do, and all sorts of factors. Relating the problem strictly to the job of the supervisory manager, it depends upon his ability to control the efficiency of labour, the use of materials, the utilization of plant and equipment, and so on. All this comes back to the effective use of capital.

From an accounting point of view, profit is the difference between the costs of the commodities and the selling prices of those com-modities. Since business is competitive, it is not merely a matter of making sure that your selling prices more than cover the costs. Rather, it is a matter of controlling costs to see that they are kept below selling prices, which, like the market prices of shares, are very much determined by supply and demand.

On the chart we have made profit. What do we do with it? First, we have to pay tax. Corporation Tax is levied on a company's

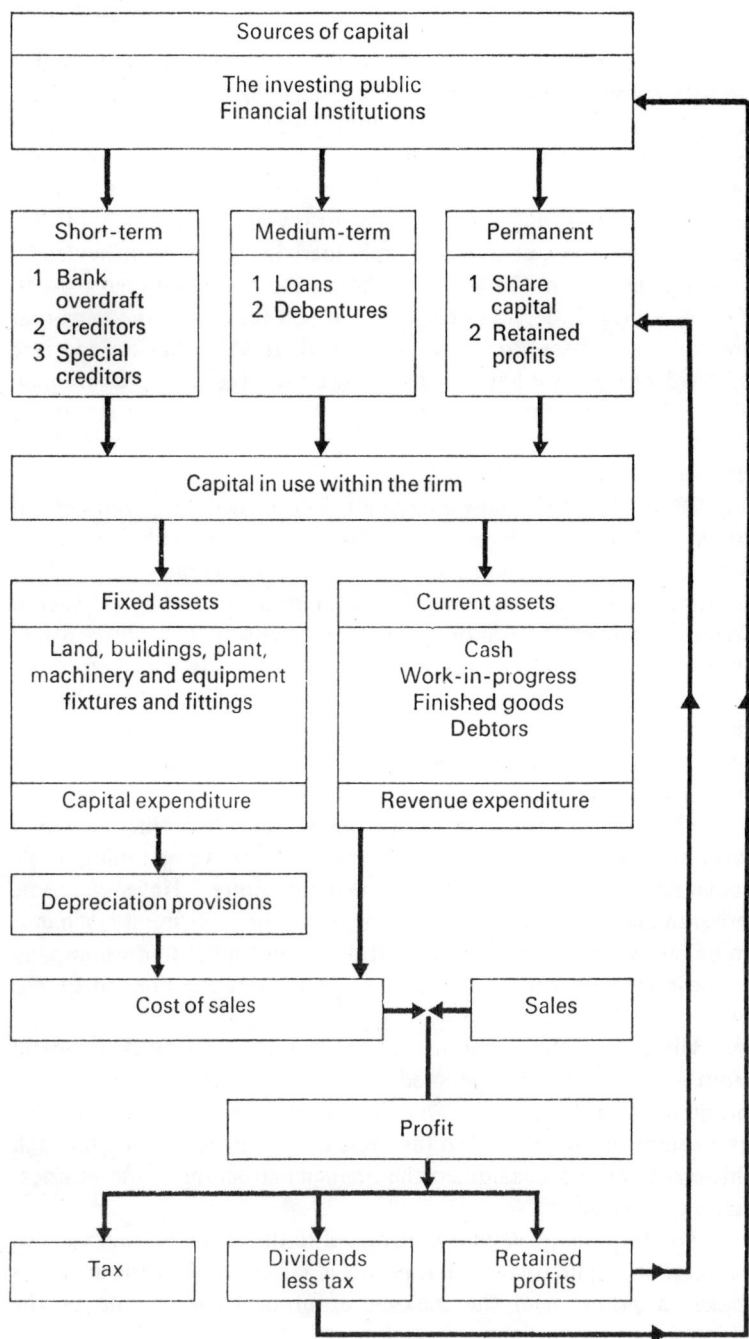

FIG. 2. *Use of capital*

profits at the rate of 40%, that is, at the rate of 40p in the pound, a pretty sizeable chunk. It is right to consider the tax bill first, because it is the first charge on a company's profit—we cannot escape it. Follow the chart a little further. If we deduct the tax from our profits, we are left with 'profits after tax', on which we have to make certain decisions. Basically, the decisions are how much of this profit we will pay out to our shareholders in the form of dividends, and how much we will retain in the business as additional capital. This is a difficult decision, complicated still further by the facts that we may have some Preference share capital which has a fixed rate of dividend, and we have to deduct tax from the dividends we pay. This is because we pay dividends net—that is, we deduct tax at the standard rate of 38·75p in the pound from the gross amount of the dividend before we make the payment.

The rate of dividend we pay on the Ordinary shares will depend upon many factors. What is our dividend record—in other words, what dividends do we normally pay? What will be the yield, bearing in mind the current market price of £1 ordinary shares? If such a share has a market price of £3 at the moment, then a dividend rate of 15% on Ordinary shares means a yield of only 5%, before tax is deducted. Then again, what is our cash position? Profits might have been such that we would like to offer a dividend of 15% on the Ordinary shares, but do we have the cash resources at the moment to make such a payment?

Then there is the question of the amount of profits we would wish to retain, and for what purposes. Are we planning large replacements of plant in the immediate future? Have we some programme of expansion which must be borne in mind? What is to be our policy in regard to the attracting of capital to the company in the immediate future? There are some sizeable questions to answer here.

Ultimately, the decisions are made to pay so much dividend from which tax will be deducted, and to retain the remainder of the profit within the business. The chart shows the 'retained earnings' as a source of capital, and so the cycle continues. In looking through this chart, we have examined the financial structure of the business fairly completely.

To recapitulate, capital is attracted to the business from various sources. It is put to use. If this use is effective, then the business makes a profit. And the making of profit must be one of the objectives of the business.

SUMMARY

1 *What is the capital in use in a supervisory manager's department?*

It comprises fixed assets, such as land, buildings, and plant and equipment, and current assets, such as work-in-progress, into which have gone materials, labour, and many other expenses.

2 *What are fixed assets in use elsewhere in the business?*

Office machinery in the office, plant in service departments, cars for sales representatives.

3 *What are the current assets in use elsewhere in the business?*

Finished stocks in the warehouse, cash at the bank, and debtors who owe money to the company.

4 *What is the essential difference between a fixed asset and a current asset?*

A fixed asset is a relatively permanent item. Current asset items are on the move, changing from day to day.

5 *How does the cycle of working capital operate?*

Cash flows out of the business to pay for materials, wages, salaries, and other overhead expenses, and flows back into the business in payment for the goods which the business makes and sells.

6 *How does the amount of working capital increase?*

By further injections of capital or by making profit.

7 *What causes working capital to decrease?*

The making of losses, or payments of tax or dividends, or the purchase of fixed asset items.

8 *What are the sources of capital?*

Permanent or long-term. (1) Share capital. (2) Profits saved up, or retained earnings, as they are frequently called.
Medium-term. (1) Loan capital generally. (2) Debentures, in particular
Short-term. (1) Bank overdraft. (2) Creditors, that is suppliers who are prepared to allow the business to purchase goods and services on credit. (3) Special creditors, such as the Inland Revenue, to whom tax owed in the short-term can be considered as additional capital.

9 *What determines the source of capital we choose at any time?*

    (a) The length of time for which the capital is required.

    (b) The costs of capital from various sources.

    (c) The extent to which the proprietors are prepared to spread the net of shareholding.

10 *What are the essential differences between the two main classes of share capital?*

An Ordinary share is the risk-bearing type of share capital, and carries voting rights: the dividend rate is declared annually and is dependent upon profits. A Preference share entitles the holder to receive a fixed percentage of dividend; accords preference in regard to payment in the event of winding up; and carries no voting rights except in exceptional circumstances, such as when dividends are in arrears or in the event of winding up.

11 *What are the main sources of loan capital?*

Loans from banks or financial institutions and the issue of debentures.

12 *What are the main items of short-term capital?*

Overdrafts from banks, creditors, and special creditors such as the Inland Revenue.

13 *What is the supervisory manager's responsibility in regard to capital?*

A responsibility to see that capital in the form of fixed and current assets is effectively employed.

14 *What is the result of effective use of capital?*

Profit. The company stays in business.

15 *What is the result of ineffective use of capital?*

Loss. The company goes out of business.

CHAPTER 2 | **The Balance Sheet**

Accounting is often called the language of business. It is the main means of measuring and communicating business data. Business data are communicated both inside the firm, between departments and managers; and outside the firm, between companies and others. Just as a newcomer must learn the terms used in his department, so anyone in management must grasp accounting language and ideas if he is to communicate effectively to other managers inside and outside the company.

In using the English language, we often find differences of opinion as to what constitutes good or poor grammar. Similar problems exist in accounting. Some practices may be described as good accounting, others as poor accounting; and differences of opinion may exist as to what constitutes one or the other. We shall try to describe the rules associated with good accounting.

Rules of Accounting

The rules of accounting are not detailed in an Act of Parliament. The Companies Acts, 1948 and 1967, stipulate that financial statements should show a 'true and fair' view of the affairs of the company. It does not state the rules to be used in arriving at that 'true and fair' view.

Nevertheless, some common guide lines are in existence, and it is as well that the supervisory manager, in learning the language of business, should understand them. He should also be able to distinguish between the differences which inevitably occur in practice within the guide lines.

We saw from Chapter 1 that a business enterprise can be thought of as a collection of assets of various types, from various sources, and employed at a profit. This view can be connected with the two basic 'statements' which the accountant produces when reporting on the enterprise. These are the *balance sheet* and the *profit and loss account*.

The balance sheet shows the assets of the enterprise at a particular point in time, and the sources of the capital used to finance those assets. The profit and loss account shows the amount of profit obtained from the use of the assets over a period of time.

To understand the construction of these two statements, we must consider five guide lines relating to the balance sheet and a further two relating to the profit and loss account.

The Balance Sheet

Guide line 1: claims = assets. The firm's assets are financed from two sources: its owners and its creditors. The amounts of capital provided by the creditors are called liabilities. It is clear from the example of the one-man concern that the assets of the business are claimed by someone, either the owner or creditors. At the same time the total claims against the enterprise cannot exceed what there is to be claimed. We can express this relationship in an equation:

$$\text{Owner's claims} + \text{liabilities} = \text{assets}$$

This relationship holds good continuously, so that an increase in owner's claims must always be accompanied by an equivalent increase in assets or a reduction in liabilities.

The claims of the owners are the residue, equal to the difference between the sum of the assets and the total liabilities.

$$\text{Owner's claims} = \text{assets} - \text{liabilities}$$

Example. The Salutation Company has cash of £10,000, owns material that cost £6,000, and owes £4,000. We can compile a report showing this position.

SALUTATION COMPANY

Balance Sheet as at 12th July, 197X

Owner's Claims	£12,000	Cash	£10,000
Liabilities	£4,000	Material	£6,000
Total claims	£16,000	Total assets	£16,000

Note

1 The report shows the position at a particular point in time: 12th July, 197X.

2 The total of claims balances the total of assets; hence the report is known as a balance sheet.

3 The claims of the owners (£12,000) are the residue, equal to the difference of the sum of the assets (£16,000) and total liabilities (£4,000).

Guide line 2: measuring in money. The balance sheet which has now been constructed expresses in *monetary terms* certain facts relating to the assets of the enterprise and the claims against those assets. That is to say, certain facts have been reduced to the common denominator of money. Accounting deals only with those facts which can be expressed in monetary terms and in consequence accounting reports may not include many important facts about a business.

Example. A balance sheet will not report that industrial relations are very strained within the company, nor that there are no immediate replacements for several key senior managers who are due to retire very shortly.

Guide line 3: the business as a separate unit. Each business enterprise is a separate entity for accounting purposes, and accounts are kept for each separate entity.

In the case of sole traders and partnerships, there is no distinction in law between the financial affairs of the business and the financial affairs of the individuals. For accounting purposes, however, the business of the sole trader and of the partnership are held to be accounting entities, quite separate from the personal affairs of the individuals.

Example. Jack Jones is sole owner of the Jayjay Café. He withdraws for his own use £50 in cash from the till of the café. As far as Jack Jones is concerned, he is no better off and no worse off as a result of this transaction. He has merely exchanged £50 of ownership interest for £50 in cash. From the point of view of Jayjay Café, however, the position has changed, since the resources have been reduced by £50. Jayjay Café is regarded as a separate entity for accounting purposes, and the financial accounts will record the effect of this transaction.

In the case of a limited liability company, the company has a legal entity separate from the shareholders who own it. Once again, accounts will be kept for the business entity of the limited liability company as distinguished from the shareholders who actually own the business.

Guide line 4: the going concern. In accounting we view the business as a going concern, and we assume that the business is not to be sold or liquidated in the near future. This implies that the existing resources of the business, such as the plant and equipment, will be used in order to add value to them, rather than to be sold in tomorrow's markets.

If this concept were not used, the accounting reports might attempt to measure what the business is currently worth to the owner at market values. In adopting the 'going concern' concept this is not necessary, and is not attempted. The resources of the company will, therefore, be shown at their cost and not at current values.

Guide line 5: measuring in actual cost. By this we mean that assets are ordinarily entered on the accounting records at the price paid to acquire them—that is at cost.

We have reached a point which managers very often find perplexing, since we must state categorically that the amounts shown against assets listed in the balance sheet of a company do not purport to show what those assets could be sold for. If a manager wishes to know the current value of a business, then the balance sheet will *not* provide the answer.

While there is a weakness here in that the economic snapshot shown on the balance sheet always deviates from that which would be given by an up-to-date assessment of asset values, it does ensure that objective evidence is the basis for recording transactions.

An up-to-date assessment involves making estimates and it is always possible that informed people and managements will disagree as to what is the right estimate. In the absence of an acceptable system which will provide objective evidence to assess the effect of changing price levels and asset values, accountants have decided at the present time not to take any action to revise the cost concept.

As a compromise, when it is absolutely certain that asset values have increased, many companies periodically revalue their assets, and incorporate the adjustments in the balance sheet. This represents an in-between stage, and does not ensure, even in those cases, that the balance sheet shows the current value of the business.

The desire for objective evidence extends beyond the accounting problems of changes in the price level. It affects the recording of many transactions. For instance, if the company pays nothing for an item it acquires, the item will not usually appear in the accounting records.

Example. ABC Company starts a business and is most successful. It builds up a reputation for quality and reliability, and makes handsome profits. It is clear that the company is building up goodwill and if someone wished to take over the ABC Company a price would have to be paid for the agreed value of goodwill. However, this item will not figure on the company's balance sheet. Now suppose that the ABC Company decides to buy up a smaller competitor who has also been successful. The agreed purchase price is £50,000, which represents £20,000 for land and buildings, £20,000 for plant and machinery, £5,000 for stocks, and £5,000 for the goodwill of the company. The goodwill represents the reputation, location, or other intangible possessions of the purchased company. In this case, the ABC Company has incurred a cost of £5,000 for goodwill, and this will be shown, together with the other amounts, in the balance sheet of the ABC Company.

Transactions and the Balance Sheet

We have now dealt with the five major items which form the generally accepted guide lines in preparing a balance sheet and we are in a position to study the effect of a series of transactions on it.

We will assume that we wish to prepare financial statements for John Stone, who operates as a wholesaler under the name of Rockwell Trading Company. The company employs as sales manager Joe King, who has excellent experience in the company's particular line of business.

Transaction 1. On 1st January John Stone commences business with a capital of £7,000 in cash. The cash is deposited in a bank. The balance sheet of Rockwell Trading Company on 1st January is:

Owner's claims	£7,000	*Current assets*	
		Bank account	£7,000
Total claims	£7,000	Total assets	£7,000

Note
(a) The total of claims balances the total of assets. (Guide line 1.)
(b) The report shows the position on the 1st January.

Transaction 2. On 2nd January fixtures and fittings are purchased by cheque for £3,000. The balance sheet for Rockwell Trading Company on 2nd January is:

Owner's claims	£7,000	*Fixed assets*	
		Fixtures and fittings	£3,000
		Current assets	
		Bank account	£4,000
Total claims	£7,000	Total assets	£7,000

Note
(a) The single transaction has affected the balance sheet in two ways—Bank and Fixtures and Fittings. This shows that we are operating a double-entry system of accounting.
(b) The report shows the position on the 2nd January.

Transaction 3. On 3rd January Joe King decides to resign and join a rival company as sales director. John Stone, the proprietor, considers this to be a great loss to the company. The balance sheet of Rockwell Trading Company on 3rd January is unchanged from 2nd January.

Owner's claims	£7,000	*Fixed assets*	
		Fixtures and fittings	£3,000
		Current assets	
		Bank account	£4,000
Total claims	£7,000	Total assets	£7,000

Note. Since this particular transaction cannot be expressed in monetary terms, it has no effect on the balance sheet. (Guide line 2.)

Transaction 4. On 4th January John Stone withdraws £1,000 cash from the bank for private purposes (in fact, to pay for a caravan). The balance sheet of Rockwell Trading Company on 4th January is:

Owner's claims	£6,000	*Fixed assets*	
		Fixtures and fittings	£3,000
		Current assets	
		Bank account	£3,000
Total claims	£6,000	Total assets	£6,000

Note
(a) The single transaction has affected the balance sheet in two ways.
(b) We are preparing accounts for Rockwell Trading Company, as distinguished from the proprietor John Stone. Therefore, we must show the effect of this transaction to the company, both in respect of cash and also owner's claims. (Guide line 3.)

Transaction 5. On 5th January the company buys a piece of land for £7,000. £2,000 was paid by cash and the balance of £5,000 was financed by a 7-year mortgage. The balance sheet of Rockwell Trading Company on 5th January is:

Owner's claims	£6,000	*Fixed assets*		
		Land	£7,000	
Fixed liability		Fixtures and fittings	£3,000	
Mortgage on land	£5,000		———	£10,000
		Current assets		
		Bank account		£1,000
Total claims	£11,000		Total assets	£11,000

Transaction 6. On 6th January the company buys some goods on credit for £1,000. Payment is to be made in 1 month's time. The balance sheet on 6th January is:

Owner's claims	£6,000	*Fixed assets*		
		Land	£7,000	
Fixed liability		Fixtures and fittings	£3,000	
Mortgage on land	£5,000		———	£10,000
		Current assets		
Current liabilities		Bank account	£1,000	
Trade creditors	£1,000	Stock in trade	£1,000	
			———	£2,000
Total claims	£12,000		Total assets	£12,000

Transaction 7. On 7th January John Stone is offered £7,000 for his claim on the business. Although his claim on the balance sheet of 6th January is only £6,000 he rejects the offer. It is clear that the business has already acquired goodwill of £1,000. The balance sheet of Rockwell Trading Company on 7th January is:

Owner's claims	£6,000	*Fixed assets*		
		Land	£7,000	
Fixed liability		Fixtures and fittings	£3,000	
Mortgage on land	£5,000		———	£10,000
		Current assets		
Current liabilities		Bank account	£1,000	
Trade creditors	£1,000	Stock in trade	£1,000	
			———	£2,000
Total claims	£12,000		Total assets	£12,000

Note. The transaction has no effect upon the balance sheet. We are viewing the business as a going concern, and we assume that the business is not to be sold or liquidated in the near future. (Guide line 4.)

Transaction 8. On 8th January the company sells for £600 cash half of the stock, which cost £500. The balance sheet of Rockwell Trading Company on 8th January is:

Owners claims			*Fixed assets*		
Capital	£6,000		Land	£7,000	
Profit	£100		Fixtures and fittings	£3,000	
		£6,100			£10,000
Fixed liability			*Current assets*		
Mortgage on land	£5,000		Cash	£600	
			Bank account	£1,000	
Current liabilities			Stock	£500	
Trade creditors	£1,000				£2,100
	Total claims	£12,100		Total assets	£12,100

Note

1 The net effect of this transaction on the assets side of the balance sheet is to increase the total from £12,000 to £12,100— i.e. by £100. This increase in assets, or profit, is claimed by the owner of the business.

2 The remaining stock is shown at £500, even though John Stone is certain that he can sell it at a profit. (Guide line 5.) In applying the guide lines it is the usual conservative practice to anticipate losses but not to anticipate profits. If the estimated net realizable value of the stock is less than the original cost, it is customary to anticipate this loss and to value the stock at its net realizable value. Similarly, if the estimated current market replacement cost is less than the original cost, the lower value is used. The effect, therefore, is to value stock at the lowest of (a) cost, (b) realizable value, (c) replacement price.

Transaction 9. On 9th January John Stone is playing golf with an estate agent friend who tells him that two plots of land identical to that owned by the company were each sold on 7th January for £8,000. The balance sheet of Rockwell Trading Company on 9th January is:

Owner's claims			Fixed assets		
Capital	£6,000		Land	£7,000	
Profit	£100		Fixtures and fittings	£3,000	
		£6,100			£10,000
Fixed liability			*Current assets*		
Mortgage on land	£5,000		Cash	£600	
			Bank account	£1,000	
Current liabilities			Stock	£500	
Trade creditors	£1,000				£2,100
Total claims	£12,100		Total assets	£12,100	

Note. The transaction has no effect upon the balance sheet. Land is shown on the balance sheet at the price paid to acquire it. (Guide line 5.)

Transaction 10. On 10th January the company sells on credit for £600 the remaining stock, which cost £500. The balance sheet of Rockwell Trading Company on 10th January is:

Owner's claims			Fixed assets		
Capital	£6,000		Land	£7,000	
Profit	£200		Fixtures and fittings	£3,000	
		£6,200			£10,000
Fixed liability			*Current assets*		
Mortgage on land	£5,000		Cash	£600	
			Bank account	£1,000	
Current liabilities			Debtors	£600	
Trade creditors	£1,000		Stock	*nil*	
					£2,200
Total claims	£12,200		Total assets	£12,200	

Note. The net effect of this transaction on the assets side of the balance sheet is to increase the total from £12,100 to £12,200—i.e. by £100. Stock £500 has been replaced by Debtors £600. This increase in assets, or profit, is claimed by the owner of the business.

The ten balance sheets which we have drawn up can be called a series of snapshots showing, at particular points in time, the assets of the company and the claims on those assets.

In Transactions 8 and 10, the company was involved in transactions which resulted in a profit. It is useful to have a statement which shows over a period the effect of those transactions which result in a profit, and which joins up the snapshots representing the situation at particular points in time.

Such a statement is called the profit and loss account. We shall examine in the next chapter the generally accepted guide lines which apply to its construction.

SUMMARY

1 *Name the two basic accounting reports*

These are (a) the balance sheet; (b) the profit and loss account.

2 *What does the balance sheet show?*

The balance sheet shows, at a particular point in time, the assets of the enterprise and the sources of the capital used to finance these assets.

3 *What does the profit and loss account show?*

The profit and loss account shows, for a period of time, the amount of profits or loss resulting from the use of the assets.

4 *Name five generally accepted guide lines used in the construction of the balance sheet.*

(a) *Claims = assets.* The total of claims balances the total of assets; hence the report is known as the balance sheet.

(b) *Measuring in money.* Accounting deals only with those facts which can be expressed in monetary terms, and in consequence accounting reports may not include many important facts about a business.

(c) *The business as a separate unit.* Each business enterprise is a separate unit for accounting purposes and accounts are kept for each separate entity. This implies that business transactions must be separated from personal transactions.

(d) *The going concern.* In accounting, we view the business as a going concern, and we assume that the business is not to be sold or liquidated in the near future.

(e) *Measuring in actual cost.* Assets are ordinarily shown in the balance sheet at the price paid to acquire them—that is, at cost. The balance sheet does not show the market value of the business.

5 *In what circumstances is it usual to value stock at less than its original cost?*

(a) *Reduction to net realizable value.* If the estimated net realizable value of the stock is less than its original cost, it is customary to use this value.

(b) *Reduction to replacement price.* If the estimated cost of replacing the stock is less than the original cost, this value is used.

The effect therefore is to value stock at the lowest of (a) cost; (b) net realizable value; (c) replacement price.

Revenues and Expenses

In Transaction 8 of the previous chapter, the company sold for £600 cash goods which had cost £500. As a result the owner's claims increased by £100, the amount of profit obtained.

It is useful to separate the two elements in this transaction. If we examine the £600 sale in isolation, this results in an increase in owner's claims of £600 and an inflow of assets of £600. Such an increase in owner's claims arising from current operations is known as *revenue*.

The company no longer owns goods costing £500, and if we treat this fact in isolation, there is a decrease in owner's claims of £500, and an outflow of assets of £500. Such a decrease in owner's claims arising from current operations is known as *expense*.

We can express the relationship in an equation as follows:

Profit = increase in owner's claims = revenue − expenses

If expenses are greater than revenue, a loss has occurred, and the claims of the owners of the business have been reduced accordingly.

Taking Transactions 8 and 10 together we can summarize as follows:

	Revenue	£1,200
Minus	Expenses	£1,000
Equals	Profit	£200

The profit of £200 represents an increase on the original capital invested by the owners in the business.

Nature of Profit

What is the nature of the profit of £200? In everyday terms it is perhaps usual to think of profit as an increase of cash. In accounting, however, this is not the case. Profit need not necessarily be represented by an increase in cash.

If we refer to Transaction 2, the bank balance has been reduced by £300 in buying fixtures and fittings, but the business does now own the fixtures and fittings. This transaction did not affect the owner's claims, and therefore the outlay of cash has not been regarded as an expense in calculating the profit.

On the other hand, in Transaction 10, goods which cost £500 were sold on credit for £600. This transaction resulted in a profit of £100, which is shown as an increase in owner's claims. We have regarded the £600 as revenue, even though cash has not yet been received.

From these examples, we can conclude that the cash balance is affected by transactions other than those which we have called revenue and expense. We can also conclude that revenues and expenses are not always accompanied by increases or decreases of equal amounts in cash.

Where is the £200 profit held? Is it held in cash, stock, land, fixtures and fittings? The answer is indeterminate. Following Guide line 1, we know that claims must always equal assets, and in the balance sheet for 10th January we show that owner's claims have increased by £200. In order to maintain our relationships, we know that assets in general must have increased by £200 or liabilities must have been reduced by £200. The owners, as a result of profitable operations, now have an additional claim of £200 against the company. This claim is a general one against total assets, and not a preferred claim against cash or against any other asset.

This concept of profit has important implications in planning the progress of a company. We can see now that a company might well be profitable and yet have a serious shortage of cash. On the other hand, surplus cash may exist in a company which is running at a loss, particularly if the company is unable to find a profitable use for the cash.

We must now consider the two guide lines which we use in measuring profit. The first guide line deals with the problem of revenue, the second deals with the measurement of expenses.

Guide line 6: revenue is realized on delivery. A number of events take place before a sale is actually achieved. Assuming that the permanent or fixed assets are already in existence, a typical list of these events would be:

1 On 1st January stocks of raw material are obtained.
2 On 1st February an order for finished goods is received.
3 On 1st February material is drawn, and is worked upon by labour—the work is now in progress.
4 On 1st March the work in progress is now complete—the good are finished.
5 On 1st April the finished goods are delivered to the customer.
6 On 1st May the customer pays cash for the goods.

At what point in time do we recognize that revenue has been realized?

The guide line used in the measurement of revenue is that revenue is realized when the goods or services are delivered—i.e. at step 5.

It is important to appreciate that according to this guide line revenue is not realized at step 2, when the order is received, even though the company can be reasonably certain of achieving the sale. Nor is it realized at step 6, when the customer pays cash for the goods. Once again we can see from this last point that since profit is the difference between revenues and expenses, and since revenue is not necessarily realized when the cash is received, it follows that profit is not necessarily held in cash.

Two exceptions. There are two major exceptions to the guide line that delivery is needed to justify the realization of revenue.

First, when a firm is working on long-term contracts covering several accounting periods, revenue is recognized by spreading the income over the period of the contract in proportion to the work completed. This method of measurement is often used in shipbuilding or construction projects. It has the effect of spreading the revenue over several accounting periods rather than waiting until the ship is finally built, or the motorway finally completed.

Secondly, when a firm is selling by long-term instalment contracts, and there is a possibility that the customer will not complete the payments, revenue is often recognized only when instalment payments are actually received.

In the first case, revenue is realized earlier than is usual in Guide line 6, and in the second case revenue is realized later.

Measurement of Revenue

Revenue may be recognized (a) before, (b) during, or (c) after the period in which the associated cash is received.

Revenue recognized before cash is received. In Transaction 10 of the previous chapter, goods were sold on credit for £600. In this case, revenue was recognized before cash was actually received. The increase in revenue was accompanied not by an increase in cash, but by the right to collect the cash. This right is often called an account receivable, or as shown in the balance sheet it is an asset called Debtors—i.e. people who owe cash to the company.

Transaction 11. On 11th January the debtors now pay their debts in cash £600. The balance sheet of Rockwell Trading Company on that date is:

Owner's claims			Fixed assets		
Capital	£6,000		Land	£7,000	
Profit	£200		Fixtures and fittings	£3,000	
		£6,200			£10,000
Fixed liability			*Current assets*		
Mortgage on land		£5,000	Cash	£1,200	
			Bank account	£1,000	
Current liabilities			Debtors	*nil*	
Trade creditors		£1,000			£2,200
	Total claims	£12,200		Total assets	£12,200

Note

1 The single transaction has affected the balance sheet in two ways (Debtors and Cash), which shows that we are still operating a double-entry system of accounting.
2 Debtors are no longer in existence; cash is increased by £600.
3 The profit on the sale was claimed in Transaction 10 when the goods were delivered and not when the cash was received. This is in accordance with Guide line 6.

Revenue recognized when cash is received. In Transaction 8 of the previous chapter, goods were sold for £600. In this case revenue was recognized on the delivery of the goods, and at the same time it so happened that cash was received.

Revenue recognized after cash is received

Transaction 12. On 12th January a customer, Jack Jones, pays £1,200 cash for goods to be supplied within 10 days. The balance sheet of Rockwell Trading Company on 12th January is:

Owner's claims			Fixed assets		
Capital	£6,000		Land	£7,000	
Profit	£200		Fixtures and		
		£6,200	fittings	£3,000	
Fixed liability					£10,000
Mortgage on land		£5,000	*Current assets*		
			Cash	£2,400	
Current liabilities			Bank account	£1,000	
Trade creditors	£1,000				£3,400
Jack Jones (pay-ment received in advance of goods)	£1,200				
		£2,200			
	Total claims	£13,400		Total assets	£13,400

Note

1 In accordance with Guide line 6, the goods have not yet been delivered, therefore no profit has been calculated.

2 The liability of the company to Jack Jones for £1,200 is shown.

Transaction 13. On 13th January the company pays £2,100 cash into the bank, and draws a cheque for £1,000 to pay for goods bought in Transaction 6. The balance sheet on 13th January is:

Owner's claims			*Fixed assets*		
Capital	£6,000		Land	£7,000	
Profit	£200		Fixtures and		
	——	£6,200	fittings	£3,000	
Fixed liability				——	£10,000
Mortgage on land	£5,000		*Current assets*		
			Cash	£300	
			Bank account	£2,100	
Current liabilities				——	£2,400
Trade creditors	*nil*				
Jack Jones (payment received in advance of goods)		£1,200			
Total claims		£12,400	Total assets		£12,400

Transaction 14. On 14th January the company buys some goods on credit for £2,000. The balance sheet on 14th January is:

Owner's claims			*Fixed assets*		
Capital	£6,000		Land	£7,000	
Profit	£200		Fixtures and		
	——	£6,200	fittings	£3,000	
Fixed liability				——	£10,000
Mortgage on land		£5,000	*Current assets*		
			Cash	£300	
Current liabilities			Bank account	£2,100	
Trade creditors	£2,000		Stock	£2,000	
Jack Jones (payment received in advance of goods)	£1,200			——	£4,400
	——	£3,200			
Total claims		£14,400	Total assets		£14,400

Transaction 15. On 15th January goods which cost £1,000 were delivered to Jack Jones in settlement of the outstanding advance of £1,200. The balance sheet on 15th January is:

Owner's claims			*Fixed assets*		
Capital	£6,000		Land	£7,000	
Profit	£400		Fixtures and fittings	£3,000	
		£6,400			£10,000
Fixed liability			*Current assets*		
Mortgage on land	£5,000		Cash	£300	
			Bank account	£2,100	
Current liabilities			Stock	£1,000	
Trade creditors	£2,000				£3,400
Jack Jones (payment in advance)	*nil*				
Total claims	£13,400		Total assets	£13,400	

Note

1 On delivery of the goods, revenue of £1,200 is realized, after cash has been received.
2 The company takes into account the expense of £1,000 in respect of the cost of goods sold.
3 Revenue (£1,200) − expense (£1,000) = profit (£200). This is claimed by the owners.

Guide line 7: expenses must be matched with revenues. In Guide line 6 we dealt with the problem of recognizing revenue. The last Guide line, 7, is concerned with the fact that expenses recognized in an accounting period are matched against the revenue recognized under Guide line 6.

We have already been concerned with this guide line. In Transactions 8, 10, and 15 we considered the goods which had been delivered, and we matched against the sales value of the goods the cost of the same goods which had been sold. The difference we regarded as profit.

But there are many other items of expense which we have not yet examined. We need to study some of these in relation to the accounting period selected by the company.

It is usual for companies to report to their shareholders at least once during the year. In this case the accounting period might be 12 months. However, to run a business effectively, management will need reports on its performance covering much shorter periods.

Frequently, accounting reports are compiled monthly, and sometimes even weekly or daily.

Having selected an accounting period, there is a major problem in determining the revenue and expenses that belong to that period.

Guide line 6 shows how we can determine the revenue that belongs to an accounting period. We can now turn to the measurement of expense. We will assume in our examples that John Stone, the proprietor of Rockwell Trading Company, wishes to know how he has done in the month of January. The accounting period which has been selected is, therefore, for 1 month, January.

Measurement of Expense

As in the case of revenue, expense may be incurred (a) before, (b) during, or (c) after the period in which the associated cash is paid out.

Expense incurred before cash is paid out

Transaction 16. On 31st January John Stone decided to calculate the profit for the month of January. He reads the electricity meters and calculates that the company has used £10 worth of electricity in January. The electricity bill will not be received until March. The balance sheet after this is:

Owner's claims			*Fixed assets*		
Capital	£6,000		Land	£7,000	
Profit	£390		Fixtures and fittings	£3,000	
	——	£6,390		——	£10,000
Fixed liability			*Current assets*		
Mortgage on land	£5,000		Cash	£300	
			Bank account	£2,100	
Current liabilities			Stock	£1,000	
Trade creditors	£2,000			——	£3,400
Accrued expense	£10				
	——	£2,010			
Total claims		£13,400	Total assets		£13,400

Note
1 Although the electricity bill has not yet been paid, the expense has been incurred during the accounting period of January, and therefore affects the profit for that period.
2 The claim of the Electricity Board is now recognized.

Expense incurred during period in which cash is paid out

Transaction 17. On 31st January salaries for the month of £50 are paid in cash. The balance sheet after this transaction is:

Owner's claims			Fixed assets		
Capital	£6,000		Land	£7,000	
Profit	£340		Fixtures and fittings	£3,000	
		£6,340			£10,000
Fixed liability			*Current assets*		
Mortgage on land	£5,000		Cash	£250	
			Bank account	£2,100	
Current liabilities			Stock	£1,000	
Trade creditors	£2,000				£3,350
Accrued expense	£10				
		£2,010			
Total claims		£13,350	Total assets		£13,350

Expense incurred after cash is paid out

Transaction 18. On 31st January a cheque for £240 is drawn to cover rates for the period 1st January to 30th June. The balance sheet after this transaction is:

Owner's claims			Fixed assets		
Capital	£6,000		Land	£7,000	
Profit	£300		Fixtures and fittings	£3,000	
		£6,300			£10,000
Fixed liability			*Current assets*		
Mortgage on land	£5,000		Cash	£250	
			Bank account	£1,860	
Current liabilities			Stock	£1,000	
Trade creditors	£2,000		Pre-payment rates	£200	
Accrued expense	£10				£3,310
		£2,010			
Total claims		£13,310	Total assets		£13,310

Note

1 The payment of £240 refers to the expense incurred for rates for January and also for the following 5 months. In accordance with Guide line 7, we need to calculate the expense which relates to the accounting period, in this case January. The charge for the month of January is one-sixth of £240—i.e. £40—and this is a deduction from profits.

2 The balance of £200 has been paid in advance, and is shown as an asset on the balance sheet.

Has John Stone now taken into account all expenses that belong to the month of January?

After careful consideration, he decides that the company should take into account the interest which will have to be paid eventually on the mortgage, and also the wear and tear caused by the use of fixtures and fittings.

Transaction 19. The rate of interest payable on the mortgage is 6% per annum, payable on 31st December of each year. John Stone calculates that the appropriate charge for January is £25. The balance sheet after this is:

Owner's claims			*Fixed assets*		
Capital	£6,000		Land	£7,000	
Profit	£275		Fixtures and fittings	£3,000	
		£6,275			£10,000
Fixed liability			*Current assets*		
Mortgage on land		£5,000	Cash	£250	
			Bank account	£1,860	
Current liabilities			Stock	£1,000	
Trade creditors	£2,000		Pre-payment rates	£200	
Accrued expense	£10				£3,310
Accrued interest	£25				
		£2,035			
Total claims		£13,310	Total assets		£13,310

Note

1 Although the interest will not be paid in cash until December, in accordance with Guide line 7, it is appropriate to charge against the profits of January the amount of interest which has accrued during the accounting period.

2 The accrued interest of £25 is recognized as a claim against the company.

Transaction 20. Fixtures and fittings which cost £3,000 have been used during the month to achieve the profit. The company considers that it is reasonable to charge a portion of the original cost of £3,000 as an expense incurred during this accounting period. It is agreed that an expense of £25 should be charged. The balance sheet after this transaction is:

Owner's claims			Fixed assets		
Capital	£6,000		Land		£7,000
Profit	£250		Fixtures and fittings	£3,000	
		£6,250	*Less* accumulated		
			depreciation	£25	
Fixed liability					£2,975
Mortgage on land	£5,000				
					£9,975
Current liabilities			*Current assets*		
Trade creditors	£2,000		Cash	£250	
Accrued expense	£10		Bank account	£1,860	
Accrued interest	£25		Stock	£1,000	
		£2,035	Pre-payment rates	£200	
					£3,310
	Total claims	£13,285		Total assets	£13,285

Note

1 The expense, known as depreciation, has been deducted from profit. The amount shown for fixtures and fittings has also been reduced by £25.

2 The aim of depreciation is to allocate the cost of the fixed asset, less salvage (if any), to the particular periods or products that benefit from the use of the fixed asset. This aim is necessary if we are to adhere to Guide line 7, so that expenses are matched with revenues.

3 The charge of £25 in the accounting period of January is an estimated allocation of the cost of fixtures and fittings for that month. The two main methods of allocating the cost of fixed assets to the particular periods or products that benefit from the use of the fixed asset are the *straight-line method* and the *reducing balance method*.

The straight-line method involves allocating the original cost of the asset (less its estimated scrap value, if any) in equal instalments over the periods of the asset's expected use.

The reducing balance method involves allocating as an expense in each period a fixed percentage of the asset's residual book value, so as to reduce the asset to its estimated salvage value at the end of its life. This latter method provides higher charges in earlier years and lower charges in later years, compared with the straight-line method which provides equal charges in each year.

4 We noted in Chapter 3 that profit is not necessarily available in cash. It follows, therefore, that the charging of depreciation as an expense against profits does not automatically create a fund of cash out of which useless assets can be replaced. However, the charge for depreciation does result in retaining assets within the company which might otherwise have been distributed. These assets might be held in any form and thus there is a management problem to ensure that the proper balance of assets is held so that replacement of fixed assets can be accomplished without undue difficulty.

The Profit and Loss Account

We have now completed our examination of the seven guide lines which are used in the construction of the balance sheet and the profit and loss account. Up to this point we have considered twenty transactions and we have developed twenty balance sheets. The first balance sheet shows the position at 1st January and the twentieth balance sheet shows the position at 31st January. During that time the original capital invested in the company has increased by £250, as a result of profitable operations.

John Stone is pleased that his original capital has increased by £250, but he feels that it should not be necessary to draw up a balance sheet after each transaction particularly as he intends to expand his activities rapidly. He needs a statement which shows how the profit of £250 has been realized. If we isolate the transactions which affected the profit of the company we can show how the profit was achieved. These transactions, which are known as revenue transactions, are numbers 8, 10, 15, 16, 17, 18, 19, and 20.

We can arrange these transactions into a profit and loss account for the month of January. The transaction number is given against each item.

Rockwell Trading Company

Profit and Loss Account for the Month of January

Revenues	*(Transaction)*		
	No.		
Sales	(8)	£600	
	(10)	£600	
	(15)	£1,200	
		———	
			£2,400

Expenses

Cost of goods sold	(8)	£500	
	(10)	£500	
	(15)	£1,000	
		———	£2,000

		Gross profit	£400
Electricity	(16)	£10	
Salaries	(17)	£50	
Rates	(18)	£40	
Mortgage interest	(19)	£25	
Depreciation	(20)	£25	
		———	£150
		Net profit	£250

Note

1 Guide lines 6 and 7 have been used to determine the revenues and expenses applicable to the month of January.

2 Gross profit is the difference between sales and the cost of goods sold.

3 Net profit is the difference between revenues and expenses for the accounting period.

4 The net profit is claimed by the owners, and represents an increase on the original capital.

5 The net profit is *not* held in cash but is represented by an increase in net assets of the company. (Net assets = assets — liabilities.)

Our next step is to consider how the transactions are recorded in the books of the company.

SUMMARY

1 *How is a profit calculated?*

Profit is the difference between revenues and expenses, and is an increase in net assets. This increase in net assets belongs to the owners of the business.

2 *What is revenue?*

Revenue is represented by an inflow of assets, and is an increase in owner's claims. The major source of revenue is the sale of products or services.

3 *What is expense?*

Expense is represented by an outflow of assets, and is a decrease in owner's claims. Expenses are used-up assets.

4 *Is profit held in cash?*

Profit is not necessarily held in cash. Profit is an increase in net assets and therefore may be reflected in an increase in assets generally, or a decrease in liabilities. The cash balance will be altered by transactions, other than those affecting revenue and expense.

5 *Name two generally accepted guide lines used in the preparation of the profit and loss account.*

   (a) *Revenue is realized on delivery*. Revenue may be recognized (a) before, (b) during, and (c) after the period in which the associated cash is received.
   (b) *Expenses must be matched with revenues*. Expenses may be incurred (a) before, (b) during, and (c) after the period in which the associated cash is paid out.

6 *What is depreciation?*

Depreciation is the estimated allocation of the cost of fixed assets to the particular periods or products that benefit from the use of the fixed asset.

7 *Outline two methods of calculating depreciation.*

   (a) *The straight-line method* involves spreading the original cost of the asset (less its estimated scrap value if any) in equal instalments over the periods of the asset's expected use.
   (b) *The reducing balance method* involves charging as an expense in each period a fixed percentage of the asset's residual book value, so as to reduce the asset to its estimated salvage value at the end of its life.

8 *Is the item Accumulated Depreciation a cash balance?*

The item Accumulated Depreciation is *not* a cash balance. The effect of the charge for depreciation in the profit and loss account is to retain assets within the company which might otherwise have been distributed. These assets might be held in any form, and not necessarily in cash.

CHAPTER 4 | Accounting Records and Systems

The Account

We have now considered a series of transactions and have recorded them by altering the appropriate items in the balance sheet after each transaction. But in some businesses, hundreds or thousands of transactions are carried out each day. These must all be recorded in some form, and it is clear that it will be clumsy if we adopt a system of recording which involves restating the balance sheet after each transaction. If we concentrate on the bank account we see that in Transaction 1 the balance was £7,000 and in Transaction 20 the balance was £1,860. Between these two transactions there have been a number of increases and decreases to the balance held in the bank. We require a system which will enable such increases and decreases to be recorded. In its simplest form, this requirement is satisfied if we record increases and decreases on either side of an account. The transactions affecting the bank account can be recorded as follows:

Bank Account

Increases		*Decreases*	
Transaction 1	£7,000	Transaction 2	£3,000
(commenced business)		(bought fixtures)	
Transaction 13	£2,100	Transaction 4	£1,000
(put cash into bank)		(withdrew cash)	
		Transaction 5	£2,000
		(land bought)	
		Transaction 13	£1,000
		(paid for goods)	
		Transaction 18	£240
		(paid rates)	
Total increases	£9,100	Total decreases	£7,240
New balance	£1,860		

During the month of January, increases have been recorded on one side of the account, decreases on the other. At the end of the month, the total decreases (£7,240) are subtracted from the total increases (£9,100). The result is the new balance of £1,860 and the amount is stated on the final balance sheet for that month.

Debit and credit. In the language of accounting, the left-hand side of any account is arbitrarily called the *debit* side and the right-hand side is arbitrarily called the *credit* side. If the total of left-hand entries exceeds the total of right-hand entries, the account is said to have a *debit balance*. Alternatively, if the total of right-hand entries exceeds the total of left-hand entries the account is said to have a *credit balance*. In the example of the bank account, there is a *debit balance* of £1,860, since the total of left-hand entries, £9,100, exceeds the total of right-hand entries, £7,240.

The words 'debit' and 'credit' often confuse newcomers to the subject since, even in this first example, we might talk in everyday terms of having credit in the bank of £1,860. We must attempt to use the language of business and to avoid possible previous conceptions that debit necessarily implies loss, and credit necessarily implies gain. This is not so in accounting.

Double-entry Accounting

The association of the word 'credit' with gain and 'debit' with loss represents, from the accountant's point of view, only half the truth. The examination of the effects of transactions on the balance sheet showed that a single transaction affected the balance sheet in at least two ways. This was called the double-entry system of accounting, and followed naturally from Guide line 1, that the total of claims against the company always equals the total of assets.

Now examine Transaction 1. We have recorded one-half of this transaction since we have shown that the bank account has increased by £7,000. If we are to adhere to Guide line 1, we must record the increase in owner's claims of £7,000. How should this be recorded? We shall see later when we examine the trial balance that it is useful to have an accounting system which will provide a means of checking the accuracy of the recordings which have taken place. This is achieved by the convention that every accounting transaction should be recorded by a debit amount, and an equal and corresponding credit amount. Following this convention we can now complete the recording of Transaction 1, as follows:

Owner's Claims

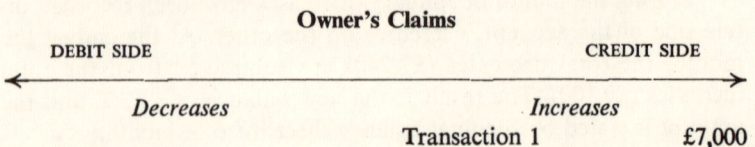

DEBIT SIDE   CREDIT SIDE

Decreases   *Increases*
Transaction 1   £7,000

From these conventions of recording, we can now develop five rules of double-entry accounting:

1 Increases in assets are *debits*, decreases are *credits*.
2 Increases in liabilities are *credits*, decreases are *debits*.
3 Increases in owner's claims are *credits*, decreases are *debits*.
4 Increases in revenues are *credits*, decreases are *debits*.
5 Increases in expenses are *debits*, decreases are *credits*.

Example. We have now developed the five rules which apply to the recording of accounting transactions, and are in a position to deal with the twenty transactions examined in Chapters 2 and 3.

The transactions have been recorded below in the accounts, which have been arranged under five main headings corresponding to the five rules of double-entry accounting listed above.

1 Assets ⎫
2 Liabilities ⎬ permanent or 'real' accounts
3 Owner's claims ⎭

4 Revenues ⎫ temporary or 'nominal' accounts
5 Expenses ⎭

Although Transactions 3, 7, and 9 represent important events in the life of the company, for the reasons already given, they are not recorded in the accounts of the company.

The accounts covering assets, liabilities, and owner's claims are often called permanent or 'real' accounts. On the other hand, revenue accounts and expense accounts are temporary or 'nominal' accounts, and represent the change which has occurred to the owner's claims as a result of current operations. This change is summarized in the profit and loss account, which, therefore, consists of revenue and expense accounts, and which represents a subdivision of the owner's claims account.

1 ASSETS

Bank Account

DEBIT			CREDIT		
Increases			*Decreases*		
(Commenced business)	Transaction 1	£7,000	Transaction 2	£3,000	(Bought fixtures)
(Put cash into bank)	Transaction 13	£2,100	Transaction 4	£1,000	(Withdrew cash)
			Transaction 5	£2,000	(Bought land)
			Transaction 13	£1,000	(Paid for goods)
			Transaction 18	£240	(Paid rates)
	Total	£9,100	Total	£7,240	
	New Balance	£1,860			

Fixtures and Fittings

DEBIT			CREDIT		
Increases			*Decreases*		
(Bought fixtures)	Transaction 2	£3,000	Transaction 20	£25	(Charged depreciation)
	Total	£3,000	Total	£25	
	New balance	£2,975			

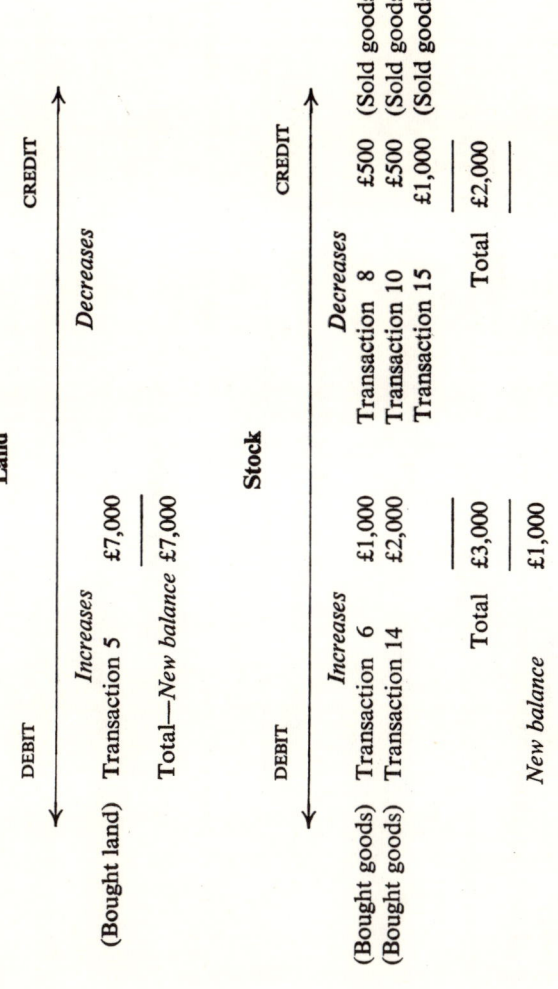

Land

DEBIT	CREDIT
Increases	*Decreases*
(Bought land) Transaction 5 £7,000	
Total—*New balance* £7,000	

Stock

DEBIT	CREDIT
Increases	*Decreases*
(Bought goods) Transaction 6 £1,000	Transaction 8 £500 (Sold goods)
(Bought goods) Transaction 14 £2,000	Transaction 10 £500 (Sold goods)
	Transaction 15 £1,000 (Sold goods)
Total £3,000	Total £2,000
New balance £1,000	

ASSETS (contd)

Cash

DEBIT			CREDIT		
Increases			*Decreases*		
(Sold stock)	Transaction 8	£600	(Put cash into bank)	Transaction 13	£2,100
(Debtors pay)	Transaction 11	£600	(Paid salaries)	Transaction 17	£50
(Cash received in advance)	Transaction 12	£1,200			
	Total	£2,400		Total	£2,150
	New balance	£250			

Trade Debtors

DEBIT			CREDIT		
Increases			*Decreases*		
(Sold goods)	Transaction 10	£600	(Debtors paid)	Transaction 11	£600
	Total	£600		Total	£600
	New balance	—			

Local Council Rates (paid in advance)

DEBIT			CREDIT		
Increases			*Decreases*		
(Paid rates)	Transaction 18	£200			
	Total—*New balance*	£200			

2 LIABILITIES

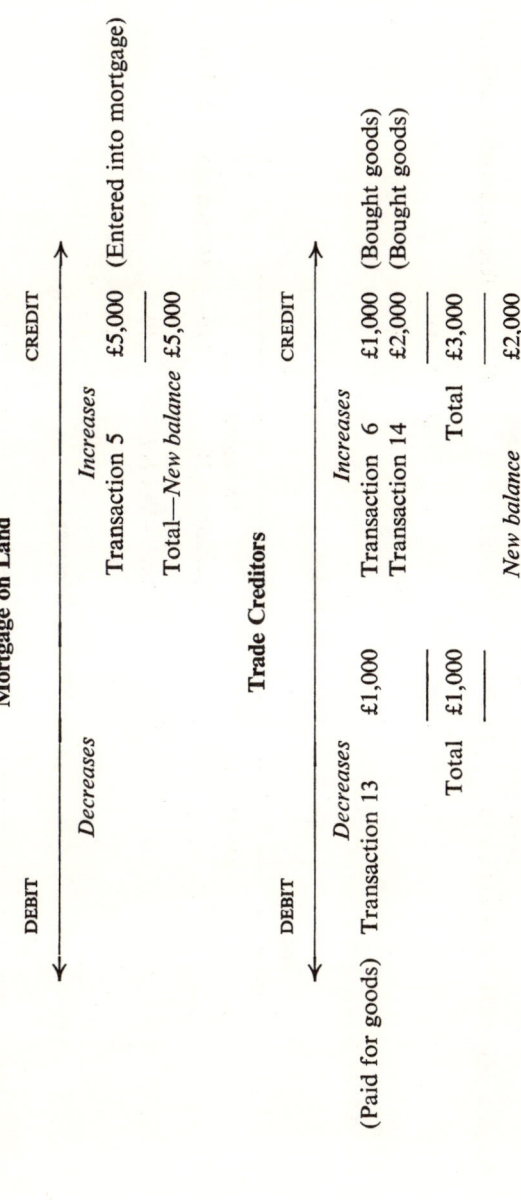

Mortgage on Land

DEBIT			CREDIT		
Decreases			*Increases*		
			Transaction 5	£5,000	(Entered into mortgage)
			Total—*New balance*	£5,000	

Trade Creditors

DEBIT			CREDIT		
Decreases			*Increases*		
(Paid for goods) Transaction 13	£1,000		Transaction 6	£1,000	(Bought goods)
			Transaction 14	£2,000	(Bought goods)
Total	£1,000		Total	£3,000	
			New balance	£2,000	

LIABILITIES (contd)

Jack Jones

DEBIT			CREDIT		
Decreases			*Increases*		
(Goods delivered) Transaction 15	£1,200		Transaction 12	£1,200	(Received cash in advance)
Total	£1,200		Total	£1,200	
			New balance	—	

Electricity Board

DEBIT		CREDIT		
Decreases		*Increases*		
		Transaction 16	£10	(Assessed electricity bill)
		Total—*New balance*	£10	

Interest Due on Mortgage

DEBIT		CREDIT		
Decreases		*Increases*		
		Transaction 19	£25	(Assessed interest due)
		Total—*New balance*	£25	

3 OWNER'S CLAIMS

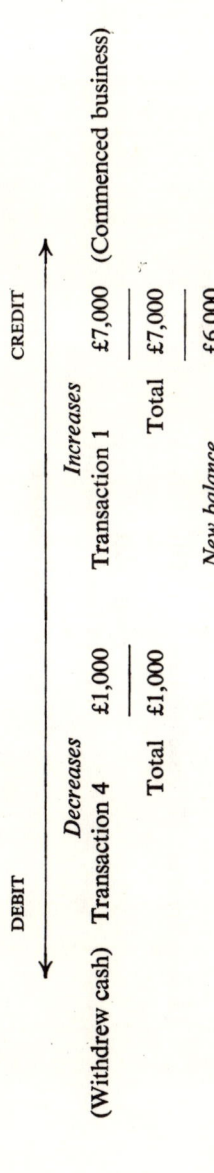

DEBIT			CREDIT	
Decreases			*Increases*	
(Withdrew cash) Transaction 4	£1,000	Transaction 1	£7,000	(Commenced business)
Total	£1,000	Total	£7,000	
		New balance	£6,000	

4 REVENUE

Sales

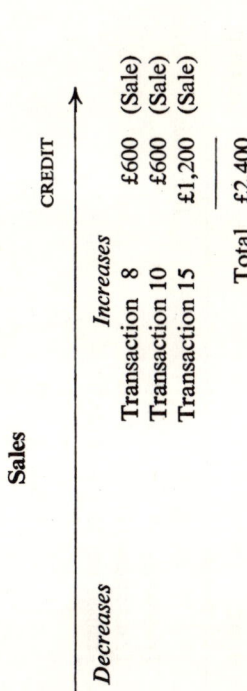

DEBIT			CREDIT	
Decreases		*Increases*		
		Transaction 8	£600	(Sale)
		Transaction 10	£600	(Sale)
		Transaction 15	£1,200	(Sale)
		Total	£2,400	

5 EXPENSES

Cost of Goods Sold

DEBIT _Increases_ | _Decreases_ CREDIT

(Cost of goods sold)	Transaction 8	£500
(Cost of goods sold)	Transaction 10	£500
(Cost of goods sold)	Transaction 15	£1,000
	Total	£2,000

Electricity Expense

DEBIT _Increases_ | _Decreases_ CREDIT

(Assessed charge)	Transaction 16	£10
	Total	£10

Salaries

DEBIT _Increases_ | _Decreases_ CREDIT

(Amount paid)	Transaction 17	£50
	Total	£50

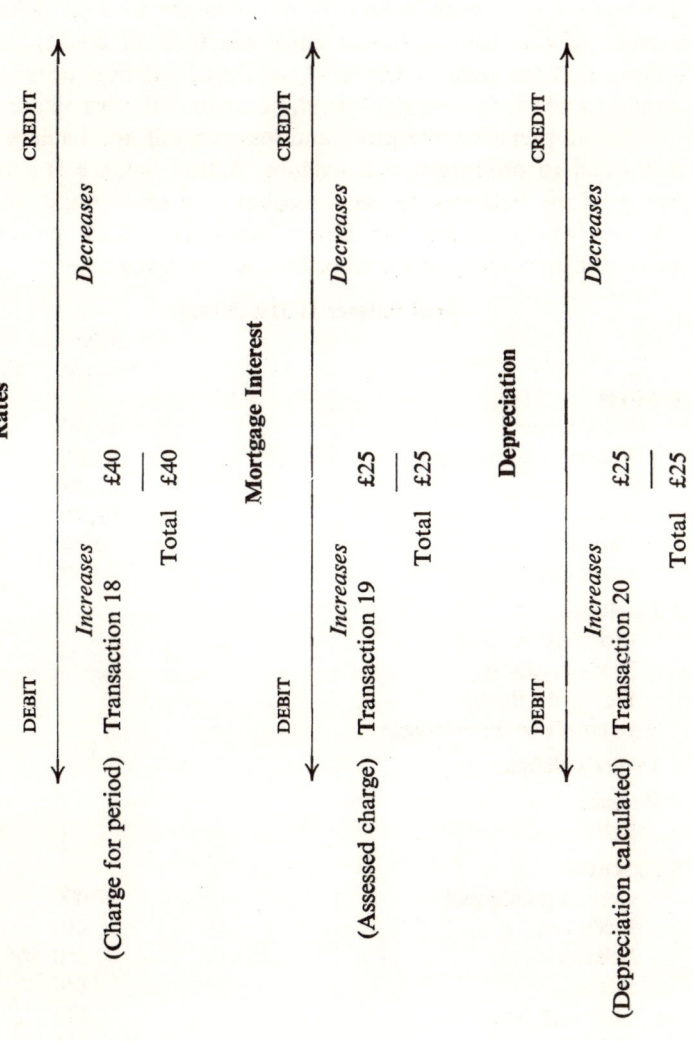

Rates

DEBIT   *Increases*   *Decreases*   CREDIT

(Charge for period)   Transaction 18   £40

Total   £40

Mortgage Interest

DEBIT   *Increases*   *Decreases*   CREDIT

(Assessed charge)   Transaction 19   £25

Total   £25

Depreciation

DEBIT   *Increases*   *Decreases*   CREDIT

(Depreciation calculated)   Transaction 20   £25

Total   £25

Trial Balance

We have now seen that Guide line 1 is satisfied by the convention that every accounting transaction is recorded by a debit amount and a corresponding equal credit amount. It follows, therefore, that if the transactions have been accurately recorded the total of debits for a series of transactions should equal the total of credits. It also follows that the total of left-hand, or debit, balances on accounts should equal the total of right-hand, or credit, balances on accounts.

Before preparing the profit and loss account and balance sheet it is usual to produce a trial balance. A trial balance is simply a listing of the balances on each account at a given point in time. The trial balance for the above accounts, which proves the arithmetical accuracy of the recording, is as follows:

Trial Balance at 31st January

	Debit balance	Credit balance
1 Assets		
Bank account	£1,860	
Fixtures and fittings	£2,975	
Land	£7,000	
Stock	£1,000	
Cash	£250	
Local council rates	£200	
2 Liabilities		
Mortgage on land		£5,000
Trade creditors		£2,000
Electricity Board		£10
Interest due on mortgage		£25
3 Owner's claims		£6,000
4 Revenue		
Sales		£2,400
5 Expenses		
Cost of goods sold	£2,000	
Electricity	£10	
Salaries	£50	
Rates	£40	
Mortgage interest	£25	
Depreciation	£25	
	£15,435	£15,435

Closing Process

We are now in a position to close the temporary accounts of revenue and expense by transferring the balances to the profit and loss account.

4 REVENUE

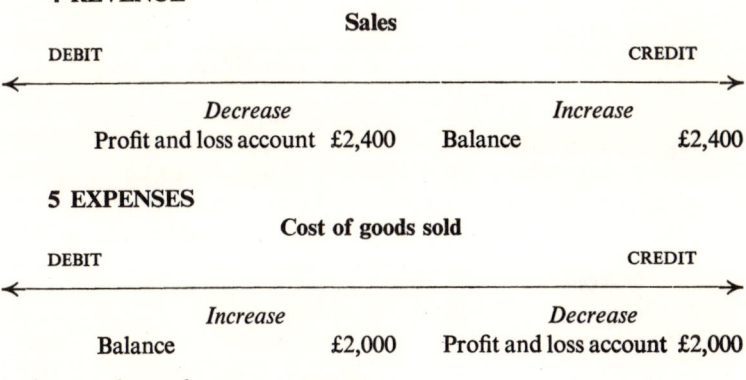

Sales

DEBIT		CREDIT	
Decrease		*Increase*	
Profit and loss account	£2,400	Balance	£2,400

5 EXPENSES

Cost of goods sold

DEBIT		CREDIT	
Increase		*Decrease*	
Balance	£2,000	Profit and loss account	£2,000

and so on for each expense account.

Profit and Loss Account for the Month of January

DEBIT			CREDIT	
Decrease			*Increase*	
5 Expenses			**4 Revenue**	
Cost of goods sold	£2,000		Sales	£2,400
Electricity	£10			
Salaries	£50			
Rates	£40			
Mortgage interest	£25			
Depreciation	£25			
Total	£2,150			£2,400
			Balance net profit	£250

The closing process is completed by transferring the balance on the profit and loss account (£250) to the owner's claims account. The balance sheet can then be prepared as follows:

Balance Sheet as at 31st January

Assets

Fixed assets

Land	£7,000	
Fixtures and fittings . . .	£2,975	
		£9,975

Current assets

Bank account	£1,860	
Cash	£250	
Stock	£1,000	
Local council rates . . .	£200	
		£3,310

Total assets   £13,285

which are financed by:

Owners

Original capital	£6,000	
Net profit	£250	
		£6,250

Fixed liability

Mortgage on land . . .	£5,000

Current liabilities

Accrued mortgage interest . .	£25	
Electricity Board	£10	
Trade creditors	£2,000	
		£2,035

Total claims   £13,285

Note

1 The balance sheet has been arranged in a vertical form. This presentation is often used in published company accounts.

2 The 'fixed' and 'current' items of assets and liabilities have been distinguished.

3 Current assets (£3,310) minus current liabilities (£2,035) equals working capital (£1,275).

Ledger and Journal

A ledger is a group of accounts, and the grouping of accounts will be determined by the complexities of the record keeping. In a small company, all accounts could be kept in one ledger. In a large company similar types of accounts may be dealt with in separate ledgers.

In these days of accounting machines and computers, a ledger might consist not only of a bound book, but also of a set of loose-leaf pages, a set of punched cards, or a magnetic tape.

In earlier days it was usual to record all transactions in chronological order in a book called the journal. The next step was to post the necessary debits and credits to the ledger accounts. Thus the journal was not an integral part of the double-entry system, but all accounting records were derived from it. With the use of office machinery and its ability to make a number of recordings simultaneously, the journal has been replaced to a large extent by other routines. It is still used, however, to record unusual transactions which are not covered by the prescribed routines.

SUMMARY

1 *What are the rules of double-entry accounting?*

The rules of double-entry accounting are:

(a) Increases in assets are *debits*, decreases are *credits*.

(b) Increases in liabilities are *credits*, decreases are *debits*.

(c) Increases in owner's claims are *credits*, decreases are *debits*.

(d) Increases in revenues are *credits*, decreases are *debits*.

(e) Increases in expenses are *debits*, decreases are *credits*.

2 *Distinguish between 'permanent' or 'real' accounts and 'temporary' or 'nominal' accounts.*

(a) The accounts covering assets, liabilities, and owner's claims are often called 'permanent' or 'real' accounts.

(b) Revenue accounts and expense accounts are often called 'temporary' or 'nominal' accounts, and represent the change which has occurred to the owner's claims as a result of current operations. This change is summarized in the profit and loss account, which therefore consists of revenue and expense accounts, and which represents a temporary sub-division of the owner's claims account.

3 *What is a trial balance?*

The trial balance is a list of the balances in each account at a given point of time. Since the double-entry accounting system has been used, the total of debit balances should equal the total of credit balances. The trial balance shows whether this equality has been maintained, and forms a convenient basis for the preparation of financial statements.

4 *What is a ledger?*

A ledger is a group of accounts.

CHAPTER 5 | Analysing Financial Statements

Let us now recapitulate on two points. First, we have said that accounting is often called the language of business, and is the main means of measuring and communicating business data. This suggests that the people running a business depend upon good accounting for reports on how the business is faring. Then, secondly, we have looked briefly at the two basic financial statements which the accountant produces when reporting upon the enterprise, namely, the balance sheet and the profit and loss account. What we have not done is to bring these two points together—in other words, we have not seen precisely how these two statements measure the success of the business in financial terms. You may disagree with this comment. You may say that the balance sheet at which you have looked has detailed the assets and liabilities of the business, and the profit and loss account has told you what has been sold, how much these sales cost, and therefore, how much profit the business has made. True, but is this enough? Have you yet a measure by which you can judge the success or otherwise of your business? No, not unless you analyse the figures in these financial statements and also take out a few meaningful ratios.

You may not have heard of the company known as Oliver Twist Limited, of London, but it is a well-known manufacturing business supplying catering utensils, including soup spoons. It was incorporated in 1922 and became a public company in 1932. You might not be quite clear what this means. Well, it means quite simply that the company was originally registered with the Registrar of Companies in 1922, as a private company. Being a private company merely implies that the number of shareholders is kept below 50, and therefore there is a restriction on the distribution of shares: public issues of shares are not made. The company 'went public' in 1932. What actually happened was that the directors needed more capital than they could provide themselves, so they approached the Registrar of Companies to increase their authorized capital. Having done this they made a public issue of shares, so we now refer to them as a public company, and we can get a quotation for their shares; that is, we can find out the current buying and selling prices. Incidentally, there used to be another important point of difference between private and public companies which is worth explaining now, because we are going to consider 'published accounts'.

Every limited company is now required to produce an annual return which it submits to the registrar, whereas prior to the Companies Act of 1967 exempt private companies were not required to submit the financial statements as a part of the annual return. An exempt private company was a private company, as already explained, subject to the additional regulation that it did not have as one of its members —that is, shareholders—a public company. Another point here is that the Companies Acts, 1948 and 1967, stipulate the content of the financial statement submitted, and if one follows the statute one is not required to produce anything like the amount of information which might be considered necessary for a proper appraisal of the business.

Now look at the most recent financial statements published by Oliver Twist Limited. You will be fairly familiar with the layout of the balance sheet which follows, because it is very similar to the one which you saw at the end of Chapter 4, except that comparative figures for the previous year are shown.

Looking through the balance sheet, we first see the fixed assets; you will notice that land is the first item and this is presumably shown at its original cost. Then there is plant and equipment, again presumably at original cost, but then subject to a deduction for depreciation. It is a statutory requirement of a balance sheet of a limited company that the provision for depreciation shall be shown as a deduction, so that the public can see what provisions are being made. Then there are some 'other assets', which are thought of as neither fixed nor current. This is a reasonable classification, since the investments are hovering midway between the two, as trade investments not being immediately realizable, and goodwill, as explained in Chapter 2, is really an intangible item—that is, it is not represented by anything tangible, such as a building or piece of plant. Then we have the current assets of the business, represented as usual by the stocks of raw material, work-in-progress, and finished products, by debtors and by cash. So the total assets employed in the business sum up to £100,000, and then we are told the sources of the finance for these assets.

You can see that all the authorized capital has not been issued. When we talk of revenue reserves, we are talking of profits saved up, some of which have been set aside (not in the form of cash) to general reserve, others which have been left as an addition to the balance on the profit and loss account, and shown as accumulated

OLIVER TWIST LIMITED

Balance Sheet as at 31st December, 1966

Assets		1966		1965
Fixed assets				
Land		£9,000		£9,000
Plant and equipment	£26,500		£24,300	
Less accumulated depreciation	£10,500		£8,000	
		£16,000		£16,300
		£25,000		
Other assets				£25,300
Trade investments		£1,560	£1,220	
Goodwill		£3,440	£3,440	
		£5,000		£4,660
Current assets				
Stocks		£42,500	£25,040	
Debtors		£27,000	£20,000	
Cash		£500	£1,000	
		£70,000		£46,040
	Total assets	£100,000		£76,000
Which are financed by:				
Owner's equity				
Authorized share capital:				
1,000 6% Pref. shares of £10 each		£10,000		£10,000
10,000 Ord. shares of £1 each		£10,000		£10,000
		£20,000		£20,000
Issued share capital:				
1,000 6% Pref. shares of £10 each		£10,000	£5,000	
5,000 Ord. shares of £1 each		£5,000	£5,000	
		£15,000		£10,000
Revenue reserves:				
General reserve		£25,000	£15,000	
Accumulated profits		£10,000	£8,600	
		£35,000		£23,600
Reserve for future tax		£9,500		£8,300
		£59,500		£41,900
Loan capital: 6% Debentures 1976/77		£10,000		£10,000
Current liabilities:				
Creditors		£19,100	£15,178	
Dividends due		£1,822	£1,822	
Current tax liability		£9,578	£7,100	
		£30,500		£24,100
	Total claims	£100,000		£76,000

profits. The 'reserve for future tax' is the amount of Corporation Tax due on the profits for the trading year just completed, which it is reasonable to regard as capital in use in the business until it is finally paid over to the Inland Revenue. The loan capital is obviously a debenture issue of some years ago, redeemable in a few years' time. The current liabilities comprise three items, the first being the amounts owing to creditors; the second being the dividends which are due but not yet paid at the date of the balance sheet; and the third being the current tax liability—that is, the amount owing to the Inland Revenue for tax on the previous year's profits.

Now take a look at the published profit and loss account.

OLIVER TWIST LIMITED
Profit and Loss Account for the year ended 31st December, 1966

	1966		1965	
Trading profit after deducting				
Depreciation	£2,500		£1,800	
Audit fee	£300		£300	
Directors' remuneration	£8,000		£6,200	
		£24,000		£20,000
Taxation on profits				
Income Tax	—		£8,300	
Profits Tax	—		£3,200	
Corporation Tax	£9,500		—	
		£9,500		£11,500
Profit after tax		£14,500		£8,500
Dividends				
On Pref. shares, net (6%)	£353		£353	
Tax on Pref. share dividend	£247		—	
On Ord. shares, net (25%)	£1,469		£1,469	
Tax on Ord. share dividend	£1,031		—	
		£3,100		£1,822
Retained profits		£11,400		£6,678
Appropriation to general reserve		£10,000		£5,000
Addition to accumulated profits		£1,400		£1,678

This is the usual form of a published profit and loss account, starting with the figure of trading profit made during the year, but quoting the details of depreciation provided, the audit fee, and the remuneration of directors, before striking the figure of profit. Then the detail of tax on the company's profits for the year appears, and such tax is deducted from the trading profit to leave Profit after Tax. Then dividends are shown as a further deduction to leave the profit which the company intends to retain, part of which has been transferred to general reserve, part retained on the profit and loss account as an addition to accumulated profits.

Taxation

Prior to the Finance Act of 1965, the tax on a company's profits was of two parts, Income Tax levied at a standard rate of 41¼p in the pound of profits, and Profits Tax at the rate of 15p in the pound. Since that Act, the tax levied on a company's profits is called Corporation Tax and is now at the rate of 40% on profits. But there is another difference. Whereas in the days of Income Tax and Profits Tax, the tax deducted from dividends was retained by the company, under the new Corporation Tax regulations such tax deducted from dividends is payable to the Inland Revenue. This explains why there is a difference in the treatment of taxation and dividends in the profit and loss account figures of Oliver Twist Limited for the years 1965 and 1966.

Dividends

Whereas the dividend on the Preference shares is at a fixed rate, the dividend declared on Ordinary shares is entirely at the discretion of the directors, and will be dependent upon the profits made and the availability of cash with which to pay dividends. In the case of Oliver Twist Limited, the decision has been taken to pay a dividend of 25% on the Ordinary shares. The only other point which must be made here is that the dividend of 25% will not represent a yield of 25%. In other words, the shareholder is not likely to be receiving a return on his investment of 25%. It is quite likely that the shareholder will have paid, say, £4 for his £1 share, so that the yield or true return on the investment will be 25% divided by 4, that is, 6¼%. As will be evident from the details, this is the gross amount of the dividend from which tax is deducted at 41¼p in the pound, so that the net dividend in the hands of the shareholder represents a return of approximately 3·67%.

Disclosures

You will note that the detailed figures of sales turnover and costs do not appear as part of the published profit and loss account.

This is quite usual, since it is not a statutory requirement at the moment to publish these details, though there is a considerable amount of pressure from many quarters for legislation on this matter. In spite of this, many public companies not only give details of turnover and a breakdown of costs, but go further in supplying a wide range of general financial statistics, such as the profits coming from different groups of products, manpower details, and a breakdown of turnover to home and export markets.

We cannot carry out a complete analysis of the financial statements of Oliver Twist Limited unless we have some information on sales turnover and costs, so that these additional details are supplied below:

	1966	1965
Sales	£180,000	£165,000
Costs of Sales		
Materials	£90,000	£80,000
Labour	£18,000	£17,000
Other Expenses	£48,000	£48,000
	£156,000	£145,000
Trading Profit	£24,000	£20,000

Measures of Profitability

What is the ultimate measure of success in a business? You might well say—the amount of profit made. On the other hand, one can imagine a situation where two businesses made the same profit but were not equally productive from the profitability point of view.

One might go on to suggest that the ultimate measure of success is the ratio of profit to capital employed. On the other hand, there are really two quite separate elements to this ratio. In the first instance, the capital is used to produce commodities for sale, so that one feature which will be of interest is the extent to which that capital is turned over in the course of a year. Then there is the question as to what rate of profit is earned on the sales. So that we can sum it up in terms of the three ratios:

$$\frac{\text{Profit}}{\text{Capital employed}} \qquad \frac{\text{Profit}}{\text{Sales}} \qquad \frac{\text{Sales}}{\text{Capital employed}}$$

which can be linked in the following way:

$$\frac{\text{Profit}}{\text{Capital employed}} = \frac{\text{Profit}}{\text{Sales}} \times \frac{\text{Sales}}{\text{Capital employed}}$$

Let us illustrate this by reference to the figures of Oliver Twist Limited. It is usual to take as the profit figure Trading Profit before Tax which for 1966 was £24,000. By reference to the balance sheet we know the total capital employed to have been £100,000 at the end of 1966. Sales turnover for 1966 was £180,000. If we take these figures as the base figures for our ratios then the ratios would be as follows:

$$\frac{\text{Profit}}{\text{Capital employed}} = \frac{£24,000}{£100,000} = 24\%$$

$$\frac{\text{Profit}}{\text{Sales}} = \frac{£24,000}{£180,000} = 13\cdot33\%$$

$$\frac{\text{Sales}}{\text{Capital employed}} = \frac{£180,000}{£100,000} = 1\cdot8$$

What do these three ratios mean? The *profit to capital employed* ratio means that for every £100 of assets in use in the business, the business earns £24 of operating profits. This formula can be adjusted in many different ways—for instance, profit can be related to the tangible assets only, by deducting goodwill. As another possibility, the interest on the debentures could be added back, so that it would be possible to relate profit before interest on loan capital to equity capital—that is, the shareholders' capital only. Again, there might be an argument for relating profit after tax to the total capital employed, since where the amount of capital investment varied from year to year, so would the tax liability vary.

Then there is the ratio of *profit to sales*. This ratio means that for every £1 of sales the business makes a net operating profit of 13p. This ratio helps in appraising the efficiency of the business operations, although fluctuations in sales price and sales volume may limit the reliability of the measure.

The implication of the *sales to capital employed* ratio is that the capital is turned over 1·8 times in a year in the form of sales going out of the business.

Having established these ratios, how can we tell whether the business is successful or not? We must be clear that financial ratios are similar to any other measuring instrument, such as a thermometer. We use them to take the temperature of a business. As with a thermometer, they give only one part of the diagnosis and they must be interpreted in the light of the other known circumstances. The ratios are merely comparative, they are not ends in themselves and considerable care must be taken in using them. On its own, any single ratio can be misleading. However, ratios do help one to ask the right sort of question when trying to establish business performance.

In evaluating the performance of Oliver Twist Limited, we must continue from the ratios which we have calculated to ask:

(a) Over the years, are the ratios improving or deteriorating? Is progress being made to improve financial performance?

(b) How does the performance compare with that of other companies in the same line of business?

(c) How does the performance compare with business organizations generally?

(d) Have we any budgets with which to compare the performance? Apart from evaluating the past in this particular way, have we budgets which we can use as targets and measures for the future?

We can do no more than compare the last 2 years' ratios of Oliver Twist Limited. They work out as follows:

	1966	1965
$\dfrac{\text{Profit}}{\text{Capital employed}}$	24%	26·3%
$\dfrac{\text{Profit}}{\text{Sales}}$	13·33%	12·1%
$\dfrac{\text{Sales}}{\text{Capital employed}}$	1·8	2·2

Over the 2 years, the ratio of profit to capital employed has diminished, though one might say only marginally. On the other hand, the ratio of profit to sales has increased, though once again only marginally. Put these two factors together and we find that the turnover of capital has diminished considerably—in fact, from 2·2 to 1·8. This is now worth following a little further. What has happened? Perhaps we are following a programme of considerable additional investment: this is borne out by the comparative figures in the balance sheet, though it is noticeable that the additional investment is in the current assets area. Turnover has not increased in proportion to this additional investment, so does this mean that there is a change in our sales and/or production policy? This sort of thing can happen when a business changes from flow production of large-volume items to batch production of small-volume items. Funnily enough, the profit per unit of sale has improved, and it often does when we change from long-run orders to short-run orders as a matter of deliberate policy to get out of the competitive large-volume work. Investigation can and should be pursued, because we must be aware where our company is going. Changes in ratios such as the ones illustrated above are not always changes which we planned; sometimes they are accidental and it is as well that we know.

A comparison with other companies is desirable. We will probably be able to get all the figures we want for public companies in the same line of business, though it is true that they will not all supply sales turnover details. There is no problem in making a comparison of our business with public companies generally. There is no difficulty in acquiring the figures we need for such nationally known names as Marks and Spencers, Woolworths, ICI, British Leyland, and hundreds of others. After having made a comparison with other companies we should be asking ourselves questions such as:

1 Why do other companies make a better return or a better profit margin on sales, or a better turnover of capital than we do?

2 Would we be better looking for a new product or a new market or getting into a new line of business altogether?

Measures of Liquidity

One of the objectives of business activity is to make a profit, but another objective which ranks alongside this is to keep sufficiently liquid, or remain solvent. There are certain ratios which can be used to test the success of an organization in reaching this particular objective. These can be summarized as follows:

(a) The ratio of current assets to current liabilities.

(b) What is often called the acid test ratio of quick assets to current liabilities.

(c) The ratio of stocks to sales.

(d) The ratio of debtors to sales.

There are other ratios, but these will suffice. Let us examine them.

First of all, the ratio of *current assets to current liabilities*. This ratio is a measure of the margin of safety of the business against unforeseen events. In the case of Oliver Twist Limited, this ratio is as follows:

$$1965 \quad \frac{\text{Current assets}}{\text{Current liabilities}} = \frac{£46,040}{£24,100} = 1\cdot91$$

$$1966 \quad \frac{\text{Current assets}}{\text{Current liabilities}} = \frac{£70,000}{£30,500} = 2\cdot29$$

The ratio is improving, and at first sight this is a good sign, particularly since it is common practice to think of a ratio of 2 to 1 as being a satisfactory measure. On the other hand, it must be understood that a company's ability to meet its day-to-day obligations depends to a large extent upon the quality and character of its current assets rather than on the total of them.

It is because of this point about the character of current assets that the acid test ratio of *quick assets to current liabilities* is often calculated. Let us see how Oliver Twist Limited is faring on this basis. By the way, when we talk of quick assets we mean those assets which are cash or near cash. In other words, in the case of Oliver Twist Limited, this would be debtors and cash.

$$1965 \quad \frac{\text{Quick assets}}{\text{Current liabilities}} = \frac{£21,000}{£24,100} = 0\cdot87$$

$$1966 \quad \frac{\text{Quick assets}}{\text{Current liabilities}} = \frac{£27,500}{£30,500} = 0\cdot9$$

Again, this ratio which tests liquidity is showing improvement. Since this ratio concentrates on cash and near-cash assets, whose value is fairly certain, it gives a clearer indication of the ability of a business to pay its immediate obligations. Common practice is to think of a ratio of below 1 to 1 as indicating some liquidity difficulty. It will be fairly obvious that the liquidity difficulty in this case is essentially one of stocks: so much of the total current assets figure was stocks.

If we now look at stocks more closely, we might test the movement of these by relating them to sales. Not that the whole of the stocks figure will necessarily be finished stock, but on the other hand one would expect stocks to be related in some way to throughput. If we calculate the ratio of *sales to stock* for the two years, the following figures emerge:

$$1965 \quad \frac{\text{Sales}}{\text{Stocks}} = \frac{£165,000}{£25,040} = 6\cdot6$$

$$1966 \quad \frac{\text{Sales}}{\text{Stocks}} = \frac{£180,000}{£42,500} = 4\cdot2$$

The implication of these figures is that the sales to stock ratio is deteriorating rather rapidly. Why should this be? It could be the rather indiscriminate and unplanned increase of stocks to meet a projected increase in sales which had not materialized. If so, then corrective action might be called for. The ratio is an indication of the rapidity with which merchandize moved through the business, and usually the higher the turnover the better the performance of the company. This is just part of the liquidity story of a business.

We have also mentioned the ratio of *debtors to sales,* and an examination of this reveals another part of the liquidity diagnosis. This ratio relates the debtors to the sales from which they arose, as follows in the case of Oliver Twist Limited.

$$1965 \quad \frac{\text{Debtors}}{\text{Sales}} = \frac{£20,000}{£165,000} = 0\cdot121$$

$$1966 \quad \frac{\text{Debtors}}{\text{Sales}} = \frac{£27,000}{£180,000} = 0\cdot15$$

It follows from these ratios that debtors are increasing in relation to the sales turnover. It seems to be taking longer to get the money in from customers. If we express it in terms of the number of days required to collect sales income, then in 1965 this would be $0\cdot121 \times 365$ days $= 44$ days. In 1966, it would calculate as $0\cdot15 \times 365$ days $= 55$ days. This could well represent a serious deterioration in the company's ability to collect its debts.

Conclusions

Certain ratios of profitability and liquidity have been calculated to enable us to measure certain aspects of a company's financial performance. Again, it must be stressed that the ratios must be interpreted and acted upon where action is called for.

Some of the limitations of ratios will have made themselves apparent *en route.* If we illustrate this by reference to the last ratio which was calculated, namely that of debtors to sales, it will be clear that such a ratio calculated at year end could be considerably distorted by violent fluctuations in sales throughout the accounting period. Then, let us refer back to the first ratio calculated, that of profit to capital employed. In calculating this ratio, we took profit for the year and related it to the capital employed figure at the end of the year. It could well be argued that the profit should be related to the average capital employed in the year, and if this were done the resultant ratios would be very different. This, however, does not invalidate the argument that measures are needed, but their limitations must be recognized.

SUMMARY

1 *What do ratios tells us, and how do they help us in running a business?*

They give us measures of how the business is faring. They act like a thermometer in giving one part of a diagnosis.

2 *What is the ultimate measure of success of a business?*

The ratio of profit to capital employed.

3 *What are the two constituent parts to the return on capital employed ratio?*

The two parts are (1) the ratio of profit to sales, and (2) the ratio of sales to capital employed.

4 *What does the ratio of sales to capital employed tell us?*

It tells us the number of times the capital is turned over during the period.

5 *What ratios give us a measure of liquidity?*

The prime ratios are those of (a) current assets to current liabilities, and (b) quick assets to current liabilities, though others such as (c) stocks to sales, and (d) debtors to sales are useful in addition.

6 *What do liquidity ratios tell us?*

They give an indication of the ability of the business to pay its way, and how effective the business is in those factors which seriously influence liquidity, such as control of inventories and control of credit.

7 *How do we use ratios?*

Ratios stimulate the asking of the right sorts of question in the endeavour to establish business performance. We watch the trends of ratios and we compare them with other organizations.

8 *What action should ratios bring?*

Action to correct unfavourable trends.

9 *What are the limitations of ratios?*

They are not ends in themselves: they merely represent the relationship between two figures. The bases, it can be argued, are not always sufficiently accurate. For example, one often relates period figures to year-end figures.

CHAPTER 6 | Accounting for Management Control

Limitations of Financial Statements

We have now taken a close look at financial statements and their analysis. How useful are such statements for managerial purposes? Distributed to managers, they can highlight certain balance sheet activities, such as stock levels. But they are somewhat limited, both as regards time and detail. Time, because people in management cannot wait until the year end to discover the results of their labours. There must be more regular reporting. Detail, because these financial statements report the activities of the business as a whole, and individual managers will probably be concerned with individual departments and groups of products. The limitations of time can be removed by the division of the accounting year into monthly or 4-weekly interim accounting periods, and the limitations of detail can be eliminated by providing the detail.

Interim Departmental Accounts

Imagine a company divides its accounting year into thirteen 4-weekly periods, and can readily break down its trading activities into three distinct product groups. A form of interim trading statement on departmental lines might be prepared, as on the next page.

Such a trading statement gives a clue as to the results for the 4-week period in question, and the cumulative results in the accounting year to date. It also gives an idea as to the relative profitability of each of the product groups. It could be distributed to interested parties in management, such as the divisional sales managers, maybe even the works manager.

Management Process

What is management? It comprises people at many different levels in a business organization and in different spheres of activity, who have responsibility for the work of others. Look around your own organization and see what managers there are. You spot immediately some people in what is often called top management, the managing director and the general manager. Then you can see divisional managers in charge of sales division, works division, finance division, and so on. Lower down, there are people in departmental management positions, often called middle managers. If you are a supervisory manager, then you are at the bottom end of the management ladder, but you are on that ladder. You direct the work of others and you have the management process to carry out.

Trading Statement, June, 1966

Product Groups

	Agricultural equipment	Steam valves	General engineering	Totals
Sales	£82,157	£14,329	£23,094	£119,580
Cumulative	£387,228	£101,995	£150,247	£639,470
Costs of production				
Materials	£68,219	£7,806	£7,900	£83,925
Labour	£6,198	£3,409	£4,028	£13,635
All other expenses	£18,522	£6,912	£7,692	£33,126
Total	£92,939	£18,127	£19,620	£130,686
Stock increase	£15,919	£3,128	—	£19,047
Stock decrease	—	—	£640	£640
Cost of sales	£77,020	£14,999	£20,260	£112,279
Cumulative	£366,999	£107,089	£132,950	£607,038
Profit/loss	£5,137	£670 loss	£2,834	£7,301
Cumulative	£20,229	£5,094 loss	£17,297	£32,432

Whatever the business, it has goals or objectives, the making of profit, a good-quality product, customer satisfaction, a contented labour force, and many others too. Though the making of profit is of great importance, you are not likely to achieve this without some attention to the other objectives mentioned. You need a policy— that is, a framework within which to operate, a statement of how, in broad terms, objectives will be achieved. Managers take the objectives and the policy framework and carry out the elements of the management job. What are these elements? We can think of them in the following manner:

1 *Planning*. Devising the programme, setting up the organization, and preparing the appropriate methods, equipment, and working instructions.

2 *Controlling*. We now have a plan aimed at the achievement of

certain objectives. These will only be secured if we have a means of ensuring adequate progress and satisfactory performance, checking performance against the plans, and using the experience gained as a guide to future operations. We need ways of measuring, using the plan as the target and the yardstick.

3 *Co-ordinating.* The various parts of an organization have to be knitted together, the activities have to be balanced. Duties have to be allocated, and there must be a mode of working and supervising work which encourages harmony among the members.

4 *Motivating.* Of utmost importance is getting the members of the organization to work effectively and show loyalty. The implication of this element of the management job may be that pants have to be kicked periodically; that backs have to be patted; it may mean showing and using all the skills of leadership.

Can the list of elements of the management process be continued? What about delegation, for example? Well, planning implies the setting up of an organization, the breaking down of duties, and the allocation of work. This could be said to be delegation. We would all agree that allocation of duties is important to the management job: no manager can be expected to undertake all the work of a division or department himself. In fact, the success that a manager achieves is often directly dependent upon his ability to allocate work efficiently, and to use the specialist functions around him. Some managers have the failing that they just cannot use other people effectively, and are loth to release much of their routine work. This brings us to another management phrase—decision making. Much of any manager's time is taken up in problem solving and decision making. This is true whatever the level of management, though there tends to be a greater volume of more important decision making at the top of an organization than at the lower levels.

The supervisor is a member of the management team, involved in undertaking each of the elements described, and concerned with the allocation of duties. The supervisor has decisions to make, some quite minor ones on a day-to-day basis, occasionally a major one. Satisfactory relationships with workpeople, with his immediate manager, and with functional heads are significant to his success. Basically, the elements of his job are the elements of any managerial position.

Planning and control. If the business objectives are to be achieved, then planning and control are important. This implies the planning and control of many different things, predominantly the use of resources, but also of sales, production, and financial activities. You will remember that throughout the divisions and departments of the business there was capital which could be used effectively or left to lie idle. It is more likely to be used effectively if its use is planned, and if techniques are employed to ensure adherence to the plan. A selling campaign requires to be thought out—that is, planned. Sales representatives may be given quotas to sell, and their effectiveness may be judged by this yardstick; this is control. A production programme will be formulated, and production control techniques will be used to ensure the closest possible adherence to the programme. The financial resources of an organization will normally be limited, so that their use must be planned, and routines must be brought into being to ensure control of spending. What will be the units of measurement for this planning and control?

The natural units of sale are the products which the company offers to consumers, but each of these has a price. The production programme starts its life as a number of products, but can be expressed in terms of facility time, which ultimately can be converted into cost. All measurements of capital, costs, and profit are naturally in monetary terms. It is logical to measure the effectiveness of an organization or any part of it in monetary terms; to express the plans for centres within the business in the same terms; and to apply controls on a monetary basis. This is not to deny the need for planning and control of business activities in the units appropriate to the particular activity. But ultimately, the success of a business tends to get measured in terms of its use of capital resources and by the profit it makes.

Measures for Management

We have seen that the financial statements give an overall picture, and that they are capable of useful analysis. The point has been made that such statements can be produced on an interim basis and that, where appropriate, the total figures can be broken down into product groups. In both cases, yardsticks can be used as measures. For example:

(a) All the ratios mentioned in the previous chapter could be budgeted—that is, there could be target ratios at which to aim. For instance, we might decide that it was appropriate to turn our capital over twice each year and that an appropriate percentage of profit on sales was $12\frac{1}{2}\%$. Therefore, we would be budgeting a profit-to-capital employed ratio of 25%.

(b) We could have similar measures for liquidity. We could take a decision on the levels of stock and work-in-progress to be permitted.

(c) Where it is possible to analyse the activities into distinct product groups, it is almost certain that the profitability of each group will be different. Here we could budget for the mix of products which was necessary to optimize our profits and we could set target profit/turnover ratios for each product group.

Let it be clear that we are talking of realistic yardsticks, which are our policy, but which at the same time are something with which to compare, and against which to control. Management needs such measures.

The measures we have talked of are predominantly for those persons in top management, directly concerned with and close to the finances of the organization. What about measures for the supervisory manager? The supervisory manager is in charge of a department, and the measures he requires are basically measurements of *performance* and *cost*. They might follow this pattern:

1 *Performance*

(a) What output is expected of the department and how far is this budget being met?

(b) To meet this budget of output what is expected in the way of operator efficiency, yield of finished product from material input, and utilization of plant? How are we doing currently?

(c) What is the permitted rate of production rejects, and what is our actual experience?

This is not an exhaustive list.

2 *Costs*

(a) For the budgeted production programme, what is the permitted level of departmental cost and how do actual operating costs compare with this?

(b) On what specific items of cost are there variances between what ought to be spent and what is currently being spent?

Again, these two points do not comprise an exhaustive list, but they do indicate the measures needed.

How do such measures apply to the supervisory job? The ability of a company to make profit and pay its way is dependent upon the effective use of resources, capital, machinery, materials, and manpower, and much of the responsibility for this effectiveness must rest in those departments where production takes place. Here the output is produced, here the machinery is worked, here is the workmanship which produces quality, and here the many costs of production are incurred. Control of performance and cost at the workshop point, at the source, are vital. The measures are aimed at inducing control, at producing the action required to secure adherence to the original plan.

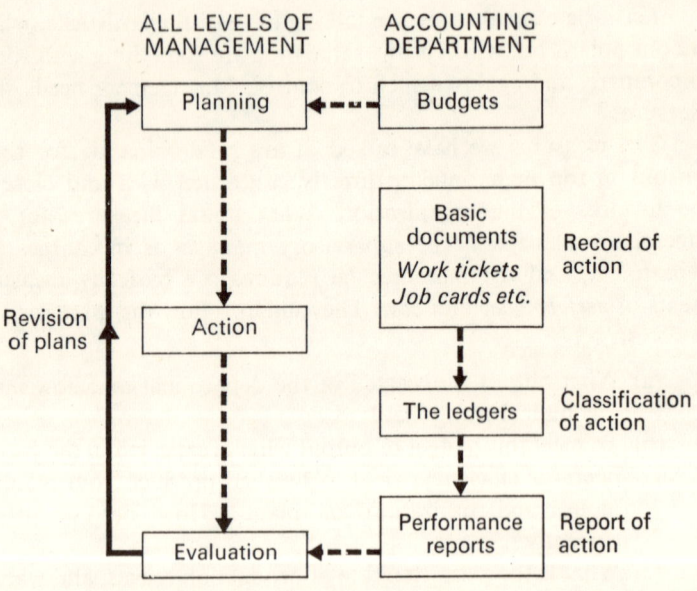

FIG. 3. *Relationship between management and the accounting department*

Role of Accountant

How does the accountant fit into the management process, and, in particular, what contribution does he make towards planning and control?

The accounting department has the responsibility for providing management with a specialized service. This service is to supply information so that all levels of management can effectively plan and control the operations of the business.

We can show the relationship between management and the accounting department by Fig. 3.

The left-hand side of the chart shows the cycle of planning and controlling by management. Management decides in the top box what is required, and also when and how it is to be carried out. The next step is to execute the plan, and to follow this with an evaluation of how well actual performance conformed to the plan. A feedback exists, following evaluation, so that if necessary new plans can be drawn up which take into account the experience already gained. 'Action' and 'evaluation' cover the management process of control.

The right-hand side of the chart shows the role of the accounting department. Management planning is expressed by the accountant as budgets. In the preparation of budgets, advice will be given about how the efforts of managers should be co-ordinated. Management control is assisted by performance reports prepared by the accounting department. To produce these reports, the accountant must record and classify actions as they occur.

The role of the accountant is similar to the function of the instrument panel in a motor car. The information given on the speedometer, the petrol gauge, and so on helps the driver to carry out his journey as planned. But, clearly, the journey cannot be completed satisfactorily unless the driver takes action, filling the car with petrol, switching on the ignition, braking at the appropriate point, and so on. In the same way, the objectives of the business will not be achieved unless management makes plans and takes action. The accountant can provide a vital service in the preparation of these plans and also in helping to design an instrument panel or control system which will aid the execution and evaluation of these plans.

In the subsequent chapters we shall look at the ways in which the accountant can assist in the cycle of planning and controlling operations. Chapter 7 deals with business budgeting, Chapter 8 and 9 with recording and classifying actions in the form of costs, and Chapter 10 with reporting and performance.

SUMMARY

1 *What are the elements of the management job?*

    1 *Planning.* That is, devising the programme, setting up the organization, and preparing the appropriate methods, equipment and working instructions.

2 *Controlling*. That is, guiding and regulating the activities of the organization to secure achievement of the plan.

3 *Co-ordinating*. That is, knitting together the various parts of the organization and balancing the activities.

4 *Motivating*. That is, getting the members of the organization to work effectively.

2 *What are the limitations of financial statements for management use?*

There are limitations both of time and detail. Time, because the balance sheet and the profit and loss account may only be produced annually; detail, because the orthodox financial statements report the activities of a business in global terms.

3 *How might some of the limitations of financial statements be overcome?*

By the production of interim trading statements, where appropriate on a departmental basis.

4 *How important are planning and control?*

If the objectives of a business are to be achieved, if resources are to be effectively utilized, then plans must be drawn up and control techniques must be used.

5 *What measures are available to management?*

All the financial and cost ratios are of use to management. Budgets or standards against which actuals can be compared are also useful measures. Managers will use many non-financial measures, such as output per man-hour and the percentage of production rejects to the total throughput.

6 *What are the particular measures for the supervisory manager?*

The measures which the supervisory manager requires are basically measurements of *performance* and *cost*. In other words, how do actual performance and cost compare with a budget or standard? A supervisory manager would be expected to act upon any differences which were revealed.

7 *What is the role of the accountant in planning and control?*

The accounting department has the responsibility for providing management with information so that all levels of management can effectively plan and control the operations of the business.

CHAPTER 7 | **Planning for Profit**

Management Must Plan

So far, we have concentrated on the problems of recording historical transactions. However, in our definition of management we saw that a major element in this job is planning, in which emphasis is on the future, rather than the past.

Just as the individual, if he is wise, thinks about and plans his future, so must an efficient management team plan the success of the business. Success rarely just happens; it is usually the result of careful planning and rigorous control in accordance with a pre-determined high level of efficiency. The job of planning is not the sole prerogative of top management; the responsibility reaches right down the management ladder—right down to the man on the first rung—the supervisory manager.

The technique which is often used to deal with this management problem is called budgetary control. This term emphasises both planning and control; a budget, after all, is really a plan expressed in quantitative and monetary terms.

In planning the success of the business, the management team must ensure that the resources of the company are used as efficiently as possible in the future. This means that they will be planning an adequate return on the capital employed by the company. As we have seen, this return on capital employed, or profit, will be used to meet the tax liability, to pay dividends to shareholders, and lastly—but very important—to be retained within the company to promote further expansion.

It is useful to distinguish two main stages in budgetary control:

Stage 1 involves forecasting and planning activities for some future period. The plans will be based on the assumption that a high level of efficiency will be attained. This chapter deals with some of the problems of Stage 1.

Stage 2 involves taking action and evaluating performance in the light of the plan developed in Stage 1. The target is to ensure that the high level of efficiency planned in Stage 1 is in fact maintained in Stage 2. This second stage is dealt with in greater detail in Chapter 10.

In Stage 1, the planning can be examined under three main

headings—Operating Budget, Capital Expenditure Budget, and Cash Budget.

Operating Budget

Two main questions which need to be answered when planning for profit are:

1 What is likely to be sold and at what value?
2 What, therefore, needs to be produced and at what cost?

The management team will be interested in the net outcome of these two questions, since this represents the profit which will be obtained by employing the capital of the business.

The *sales budget* deals with the first question and often this plan represents the starting point in budgetary control procedures. The sales forecast is sometimes likened to the king-pin of the whole structure, since all other operating and financial planning are generally geared to the level of sales.

The ease with which the king-pin can be determined will depend upon the type of product and the marketing characteristics of the trade. When a company is selling standard lines through relatively assured outlets, it is possible to forecast accurately the sales demand. In this case a sales budget covering 6 or 12 months would be quite normal. In other cases it may not be possible to plan in detail more than 2 or 3 months ahead.

However, as a general rule we can say that the sales forecast will be based on past patterns of sales adjusted for any estimated changes for the next period. The estimated change for the next period will take into account:

(a) Estimates made by the sales force.
(b) General economic and competitive conditions.
(c) Market research studies.
(d) Advertising, sales promotions, and product development plans.

The *production budget* deals with the second question, the volume of output required, taking into account the present and prospective finished stock positions. At this point it will be necessary to examine the productive capacity of the whole plant, and also the capacity of individual operating departments. Possible bottlenecks will be noted, and plans will be developed to deal with those limiting factors. It may be decided to sub-contract a proportion of the total work required, or possibly buy out certain components. The desired level of stocks must also be determined. This is a difficult problem for the management team. On the one hand, an unnecessarily high level of stock may imply poor utilization of the resources of the company. On the other hand, stock levels which permit stability in production and prompt satisfaction of customers demands are a vital factor in the profitability of a company. Continuous and patient planning of sales and production is required in order to adopt and refine a stock policy which is suitable for a particular business.

Production budgets can next be developed for individual departments. These will show the different amounts of products to be made in different periods. The budgeted cost of this production will be evaluated for each item of cost. This means that budgets are developed in each department to cover direct materials, direct labour, and overheads. These budgets are also used for cost control purposes, and are flexible or adjustable to the actual level of operations. This matter will be dealt with in greater detail in Chapter 10.

Finally, to complete the operating budget, it will be necessary to prepare budgets for all other operating costs within the business. This will involve developing budgets for administration, selling, and distribution costs. Once again, these plans will be made on the assumption that a high level of efficiency will be attained in these areas of activity.

Capital Expenditure Budget

In addition to planning activities which will take place in the near future, the management team must also plan expenditure which will yield benefits to the company over a long period of time. The problem here is the planning of expenditure on fixed assets. Outlays on land and buildings, plant and machinery, vehicles, and other fixed assets have long-term implications for the company with regard to flexibility and earning power. This expenditure, therefore, requires careful planning. The problem is double edged. On the one hand a decision has to be made as to the type of fixed asset which is to be acquired. On the other hand, finance has to be made available for the purchase. The demands for this finance must be co-ordinated with demands for finance for activities covered in the operating budget.

Cash Budget

The cash budget is used to deal with this problem of planning and co-ordinating the inflows and outflows of cash. The operating budget is prepared in terms of revenues and expenses, and we have seen in previous chapters that the balance of profit is not necessarily held in cash. We need to translate the operating budget and the capital expenditure budget into terms of cash receipts and cash disbursements. The object of the cash budget is to ensure that the right amount of cash is provided to operate the business. If there is too much cash, this may imply poor utilization of the resources of the company. If there is too little cash, it may be necessary to restrict current operations, and to forego projects involving capital expenditure.

Advantages of Budgets

It will be useful to summarize the advantages of this first stage of planning in a budgetary control system.

1 The managers of a business are responsible for the efficient use of capital entrusted to them by the owners. Budgeting implies that proper plans are drawn up which will ensure an adequate return on the capital.

2 Managers are forced to face the future, and accept planning as an essential element of their job. All too often managers operate on a day-to-day basis, and the job of planning future activities is neglected.

3 Budgets are drawn up on the basis that a high level of efficiency will be obtained. This means that standards of performance are determined and can be used in evaluating subsequent actions.

4 The budget acts as a means of communication and co-ordination. The overall objectives of the business are communicated to managers, and provide a recognized framework in which to work. The objectives of individual departments are co-ordinated in order to achieve the overall objective. In this process, managers see their relationship to other departments and also to the company as a whole.

The interrelationships of the various budgets are shown in Fig. 4.

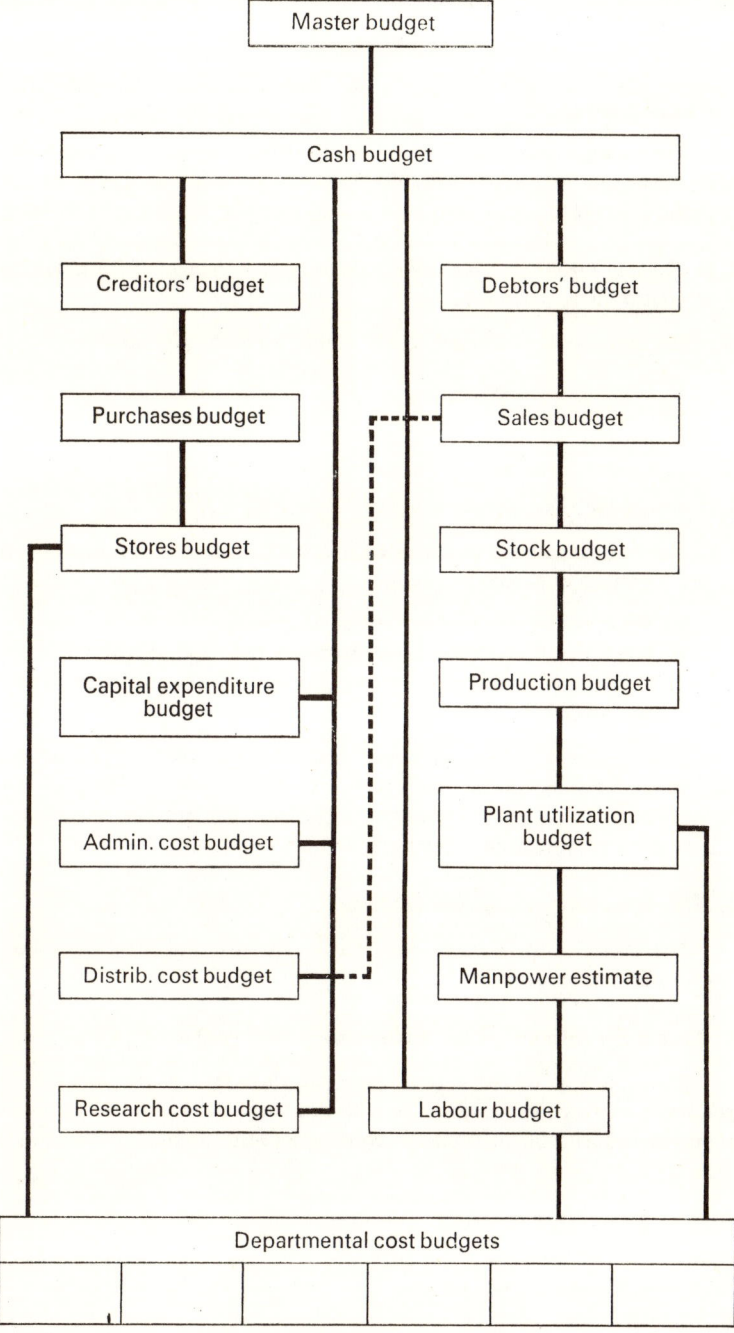

FIG. 4. *Interrelationship of budgets*

SUMMARY

1 *Why plan for profit?*

The management of a company is entrusted with resources, and one of its major problems is to ensure that these resources are used as efficiently as possible in the future. To meet the future, plans or budgets are necessary.

2 *In planning for profit, what are the main types of budget which should be developed by management?*

The main types of budget which should be developed are:

(a) Operating budgets.
(b) Cash budget.
(c) Capital expenditure budget.

3 *What are the main objects of the operating budget?*

The main objectives of the operating budget are to plan the answers to the following questions:

(a) What is likely to be sold and at what value?
(b) What therefore needs to be produced and at what cost?
(c) What is likely to be the resulting profit and the return on capital employed?

This requires the development of detailed plans for sales, production, and administration, on the assumption that a high level of efficiency will be obtained. This means standards of performance are determined and n be used in evaluating subsequent actions.

4 *What is the objective of the cash budget?*

The objective of the cash budget is to forecast and plan the inflows and outflows of cash.

5 *What is the objective of the capital expenditure budget?*

The objective of the capital expenditure budget is to plan the expenditure on new fixed assets. The plan must cover the type of asset to be acquired and also the method of financing its acquisition.

CHAPTER 8

Cost Analysis and Costing Procedures

In most manufacturing businesses of any size there is a costing function. This often started its life as a part of the factory; factory cost was the large element of cost and the factory manager or superintendent was expected to keep certain cost statistics. Often these were quite primitive, being merely a record of hours spent and wages cost on each production order which had been executed in the factory. Sometimes rough material cost records were kept in addition, but often they were no more than an estimate of the material requirements of each job. The emphasis was on what we now call *cost finding*, or *cost ascertainment*, and little or no attempt was made to practice what we call *cost control*.

The costing function in the modern business operates in a different manner. The attention of the cost department must be directed to costs in all the divisions of the business, and the activities of costing cannot be confined to material and labour costs only. There are many other costs, which we call overhead expenses, and which are now significant and merit attention. The costs of tools and consumables, fuel and power, salaries, rates, and general administrative expenses are such as to need accounting for and to be kept under observation.

Further, the activities cannot be restricted to finding what the costs are and where they are incurred. The cost department is expected to play an active part in the attempts to control cost and reduce it, wherever possible.

If costing is to be done accurately, the cost department must be a part of the accounting division of a business organization. There are two reasons for this. Firstly, the cost department relies for its information on accounting data, the purchase and sales invoices, and the payroll, while the cash and petty cash vouchers used for financial accounting records require to be further analysed so that departmental cost figures can be extracted. Access to these documents must be available to costing personnel. Secondly, if the clerical work and data processing of a business is to be done economically and efficiently, then it needs to be done once, comprehensively, for all purposes.

Role of Supervisory Manager

The role of the supervisory manager in costing is quite logical. He is in charge of a department, a business within a business; this department incurs cost, and the supervisor has a cost responsibility, namely to keep the costs of his department within bounds, and to endeavour by all possible means to eliminate or reduce costs.

Know your costs. First of all, a supervisory manager should know what his costs are, and what are the significant costs. How can a supervisory manager accept the responsibility for costs without knowledge of their nature?

To convey this knowledge there must be a service of cost information to the supervisor, and the costing function will be responsible for providing this. If this cost information is to be accurate and reliable, the supervisory manager must have interested himself in the basic costing routines which apply to his own department. Much of the basic cost information analysed and collated in the cost department stems from the shop floor. This cost information comes from time sheets and piecework tickets, stores requisitions, and the like. Without accurate data on these matters, a reliable cost information service is not possible.

The supervisory manager must:

1 Insist on having prompt and reliable cost information to assist him in running his department.
2 Pay attention to basic costing routines and the accuracy of vouchers to ensure the accuracy of cost data.
3 Encourage co-operation with the costing function to extract the maximum benefit from the service.

Cost Analysis

If the supervisory manager is to know what his costs are, then there must be proper costing procedures based upon cost analysis.

For cost analysis purposes, business expenditure may be classified in several different ways, which we will now examine. First of all, costs may be divided into three main groups as follows:

1 *Material cost.* The costs of all materials and components supplied to an undertaking, whether or not they form part of the finished product, are material costs.
2 *Wages.* These are the costs of remunerating the employees of an undertaking whether by wages, salaries, commissions, or bonuses.

3 *Expenses.* Apart from material costs and wages, there are many other expenses. These are largely the costs of services provided to a business, and the notional costs of the use of the assets, that is, the land, buildings, plant, and equipment.

We can then divide each of these three groups into *direct* and *indirect* items of cost. The implication of the word 'direct' is that some items of cost are capable of being allocated direct to the ultimate *cost unit.* When we talk of a cost unit we mean the product, job, or order. Examples of such direct costs now follow.

Direct material cost. This is that part of the total material cost which can be attributed directly to cost units or the finished product. Any material which is purchased specially for a particular job or product, or which is purchased for stock and issued to a particular job or product, can be called the direct material of that job. Bought-out components which are assembled into the product in the factory are direct materials of that product.

Direct wages cost. This includes all those wages which can be allocated to the cost units—that is, wages paid to labour which actually contributes to the conversion of the raw material or component parts into finished products, altering either the shape, conformation, or chemical properties of the article. This is often referred to as direct labour or productive labour. The analysis of labour into direct and indirect is for costing convenience, and is not intended as a verdict on the usefulness of a person's occupation. The creative ability of the designer will be as useful to the business as the productive efforts of the machine operator. But whereas the machine operator's wages can normally be identified without too much difficulty with the product, job, or order, this is often not true of the designer's salary.

Direct expense. This is a cost, other than material or labour, which can be directly allocated to the cost unit. Two typical examples of direct expense would be:

1 Plant hired specifically for the manufacture of one particular job order.
2 Special tools bought out or manufactured for a particular contract.

We have now examined those items of cost which form a part of *prime cost.* When we talk of prime cost, we are talking of the first elements of cost. To recapitulate:

Direct materials + direct wages + direct expenses = prime cost

But there are also indirect items of cost. And the implication of the word 'indirect' is that these items of cost cannot be allocated direct to the cost unit or finished product. Usually, an analysis of these items of cost is to the division, department, or *cost centre* which incurs these costs.

Indirect material cost. This is that part of the total material cost which cannot be attributed to cost units or the finished product. The best examples are the tools and consumables used in the manufacturing or service department.

Indirect wages cost. This is that part of the total wages cost which comprises wages paid to employees whose work does not make a direct contribution to the change in shape, conformation, or chemical properties of the product. Examples of this are wages paid to shop cleaners and sweepers, maintenance personnel, inspectors, store-keepers, and even supervisory managers.

Indirect expenses. These are such items as rent and rates, power and services generally, insurance, depreciation of buildings and plant. These are costs incurred through services vital to production, but nevertheless not directly identifiable with the products.

We have now examined those items of indirect cost which, when added together, comprise what are usually called *overheads*. Overheads can be classified according to the divisions, departments, and cost centres in the business. Reference to the organization chart of the business will indicate the nature of the divisions, but they will probably be production, administration, selling and distribution.

In each division there are departments. For example, in the factory there are certain production departments and service departments. The production department might comprise a power press shop, a fly press shop, an assembly department, and a finishing department. Service departments would certainly include mainten-ance department, toolroom, stores, and power services. In the administration division, there would be the sales office, the sales force, warehouse, and several other sections. Costs can be classified according to these divisions and the departments within them. In the production departments, it might be appropriate to analyse costs even further to cost centres. For example, in the power press shop, there might be presses of different capacities, attracting quite different costs, and in this case a further cost analysis might be called for.

An example of a detailed cost analysis, showing all the classifications mentioned, is given in Fig. 5.

Let us now follow through this cost analysis. If we move

horizontally across the form, we see that costs have been analysed first of all into the main divisions of factory, administration, and selling and distribution, and then into departments within divisions. It will be noted that the factory division comprises some manufacturing departments, some service departments, and certain general cost centres. The manufacturing departments are not in this case broken down to smaller cost centres within the departments, though this can be done, if merited. If we now move down the form, we find that the cost analysis is by the various elements of cost. Each department has been given a cost centre code and each item of expense has been given an expense number code. Coding routines are essential to cost analysis. All the various items of materials, wages, and expenses have been analysed by use of the coding routines.

As an example, suppose that the supervisory manager of the assembly shop requisitions tools from stores; then the requisition would be coded 52/15. The time sheet of the inspector in the fly press shop would be coded 51/10. If the supervisory manager of the finishing department called upon the maintenance department to carry out breakdown maintenance work in his shop, then he would code the maintenance order 53/12. The dual nature of the code will now be perceived: costs are being analysed to the appropriate department and also by nature of the expense.

An examination of the various cost items will indicate that, whereas some items of cost can be *allocated* without difficulty to the departments or cost centres, some cost items can only be *apportioned* on an arbitrary or technical estimate basis. For example, if the power press shop has its own indirect workers responsible for keeping the shop clean, feeding material to machines, and taking products away, then the wages of these indirect workers can be allocated to the power press shop as overhead items of that department. On the other hand, the rates bill is paid twice a year for the business as a whole, and if this expense is to be charged to individual departments, it would have to be apportioned on some equitable basis. A satisfactory basis for this item of expense would be floor area. Then there is the problem of the costs of service departments. These costs must be apportioned to production departments also, since it is the production departments which use the services, and the production departments which make the products, which in the ultimate have to bear all the costs of the business. On the annual cost analysis sheet, the costs of running the stores department have been apportioned to all other departments on the basis of issues made,

COST CENTRE CODE	Expenses Code	Totals £	F A C T O R (cont.)						
			MFG DEPTS				SERV		
			50	51	52	53	60	61	6
			Press Shop-power	Press Shop-fly	Assembly Shop	Finish'g Shop	Tool Toom	Mtce Dept	
Prime costs									
Direct materials	01	342,577	107,603	47,102	162,862	25,010			
Direct wages	02	79,608	23,521	6,352	28,827	20,908			
Direct expenses (outwork)	03	16,004				16,004			
		438,189	131,124	53,454	191,689	61,922			
Overheads									
Indirect wages—inspection	10	13,135	2,934	978	3,955	5,268			
—labouring etc.	11	22,722	3,824	576	1,689	3,402	120	220	2
—maintenance	12	13,128	5,680	520	1,900	2,800	356	112	
—tool making	13	4,696	2,863	537	501	494			
Maintenance materials	14	15,300	9,473	327	860	2,437	275	388	
Tools and consumable stores	15	22,636	12,801	526	2,268	1,916	512	401	
		529,806	168,699	56,918	202,862	78,239	1.263	1,121	
Salaries and directors' fees	20	65,151	3.021	1,850	3,700	2,700	1,300	1,264	1
National Insurance, etc.	21	9,322	1,732	460	2,004	1,610	240	560	
Holiday pay	22	6.561	1,543	384	1,844	1,408	180	468	
Electricity	23	9,504							
Fuel oil	24	3,106							
Rates	25	6,310	1,180	330	1,710	660	130	200	
Insurance, fire, etc.	26	2,823	475	30	100	128	18	18	
Depreciation	27	40,303	17,690	509	2,005	14,510	642	293	
Printing and stationery	28	3,571							
Telephone	29	3,446							
Consultancy fees	30	2,000							
Audit fees	31	400							
Advertising	32	14,340							
Commission and expenses	33	8,418							
Packing materials	34	13,104							
Carriage and freight	35	8,221							
		726,386	194,340	60,481	214,225	99,255	3,773	3,924	
Apportionments:—									
Power service (on tech. est.)			6,266	423	2,875	4,001	665	542	
Stores (on no. of requisitions)			880	264	1,760	564	210	846	
Mtce dept (on mtce. wages)			2,756	254	930	1,372		5,312	
Tool room (on tool making wages)			2,965	590	550	543	4,648		
Total Costs		726,386	207,207	62,012	220,340	105,735			
Less prime cost		438,189	131,124	53,454	191,689	61,922			
Total overheads		288,197	76,083	8,558	28,651	43,813			

Fig. 5. *Annual cost analysis*

O S T S

Services	GENERAL FCTRY			ADMIN. COSTS				SELLING & DISTRIB. COSTS					
	67	68	69	72	73	74	75	80	81	82	83	84	85
	Factory admin.	Factory general	Design & devel.	Buying Dept	Accounts	General Office	General m'n'ment costs	Sales Office	Sales force	Advt & Promn	Ware-house	Packing	Carr. & freight
27		2,575									4,257	2,821	
)60		450										250	
			301										
60		220										160	
320		1,338	1,646								100	188	
967		4,583	1,947								4,357	3,419	
	10,420		3,628	3,460	8,800	3,550	4,000	8,486	6,000	1,822			
80	420	146	120	150	360	200	40	280	240	90	220	210	
72		134									212	208	
504													
06													
30	50	1,050	70	10	40	40		30		20	200	130	
46	5	10	15		12	8	1,606	5	6		115	24	
80	35	320	860	10	451	235		50	250	5	210	504	
	300					2,071		1,200					
	400					1,200		1,846					
							2,000						
							400						
										14,340			
							1,238	860	6,070	250			
												13,104	
													8,221
85	11,630	6,243	6,640	3,630	9,663	7,304	9,284	12,757	12,566	16,527	5,314	17,599	8,221
85	35	1,984	172	12	154	29		30		14	470	381	
					17	17					88	311	
	11,665	8,227	6,812	3,642	9,834	7,350	9,284	12,787	12,566	16,541	5,872	18,291	8,221
	11,665	8,227	6,812	3,642	9,834	7,350	9,284	12,787	12,566	16,541	5,872	18,291	8,221
		26,704			30,110					74,278				

represented by the number of requisitions. There are other bases which could be adopted, such as the value of issues.

As a result of analysing the costs of the business, carrying out these allocations and apportionments, we now know the cost of running each department in terms of the prime costs and the overheads. Of what use is this information to us?

First, we now know what our costs are on a departmental basis.

Secondly, we now know what are the various cost items, and which are the most significant. Perhaps we did not know before. If this were so, then we must have found considerable difficulty in preparing estimates and fixing selling prices, because without a detailed knowledge of cost, it is not possible to fix the cost rates required to calculate accurate estimates.

Thirdly, if we want to be in a position to calculate product costs and to evaluate the profitability of products, then again it is necessary to know the departmental cost rates.

Fourthly, costs cannot be successfully controlled unless there is detailed knowledge of them, unless the trend of costs can be followed, and unless there is a yardstick against which to measure them. Since the theme of cost control is developed fully in Chapter 10, we will now concentrate on the calculation of cost rates and their use in cost estimating and product costing.

Overhead Cost Rates

When estimating the cost of a product for selling price fixing, or preparing an actual product cost, the work of calculating the direct material and direct labour costs is relatively easy. Usually, it is a matter of ascertaining the quantities of different items of materials and components which go to make up a product, and multiplying these quantities by the bought-out prices of the items. There may be problems of material waste and scrap, where experience of the actual incidence of such losses will be called upon. In respect of direct labour, this is usually tackled by detailing the direct labour operations required, specifying the times in actual or standard minutes, and then multiplying these times by the appropriate labour rates. Note that in calculating both these prime cost elements, there is a *quantity* and a *price* aspect.

The difficulty in cost estimating and product costing is usually in the recovery or *absorption* of overhead costs. This difficulty arises in two ways. First, there is the problem of establishing the level of overhead expenditure which is relevant. Secondly, there is the problem of what method of overhead absorption to use.

Level of overhead expenditure. The annual cost analysis which we examined represents the actual expenses which have been received for 1 year, which we will assume ended on 30th September, 1966. However, we might well wish to prepare a product cost or an estimate in December 1966. The annual cost analysis covering that month will not be available for another 10 months or so, but the information is required in December. What are we to do? The answer is to prepare an estimated annual cost analysis. This estimate must take into account the level of activity or output anticipated during the whole year, and the level of expenditure appropriate to that level of output. Clearly, if the actual level of expenditure for the year, which will not be known until the end of the accounting year, is not in line with the estimate of expenditure, then the product costs and estimates used in December will have been under- or over-stated. This represents a most serious problem to both the accountant and to management, which can vitally affect the progress of a company. In our examination of the different methods of overhead absorption we will assume that the annual cost analysis represents a level of expenditure appropriate to the level of output which is likely to be achieved during the year.

Methods of overhead absorption. Many methods of overhead absorption are in use, and it would be as well to examine the most significant and popular of these. Before we do this, let us remember that the overheads are capable of a divisional breakdown, so that it is logical to consider different methods of absorbing the overheads of different divisions. First of all, we will consider factory overheads.

Factory Overheads

Percentage of direct labour rate. Sometimes factory overheads are recovered on the basis of direct labour—that is, they are expressed as a percentage of direct labour. On occasions this overhead rate is calculated for the factory as a whole, irrespective of the different departments. In our example of an annual cost analysis we have a business with four different manufacturing departments. Apart from the nature of the operations carried out in each department, the incidence of overheads in each will be different: compare, for example, a power press shop with a fly press shop. We will go no further in our comparison than to point out that the machine tools are very different in size, in cost, in the method of motive power, and in use of dies. Would it be accurate to use a 'blanket' rate of overheads covering two departments such as these? From now on, the view will be taken that we would require to calculate separate departmental rates, though there might be an isolated instance of a factory with several different departments, through each of which the products passed, where it would be equitable to use an overall rate.

Referring to our annual cost analysis, let us calculate the overhead rate as a percentage of direct labour for the four manufacturing departments:

Cost centre 50: Power press shop $\dfrac{\text{Overheads}}{\text{Direct labour}} = \dfrac{£76,083}{23,521} = 324\%$

The implication of the rate computed is that every job or product passing through this department will bear a charge for departmental overheads at the rate of 324% of the direct labour cost of that job or product.

Cost centre 51: Fly press shop $\dfrac{\text{Overheads}}{\text{Direct labour}} = \dfrac{£8,558}{6,352} = 135\%$

Cost centre 52: Assembly shop $\dfrac{\text{Overheads}}{\text{Direct labour}} = \dfrac{£28,651}{28,827} = 100\%$

Cost centre 53: Finishing shop $\dfrac{\text{Overheads}}{\text{Direct labour}} = \dfrac{£43,813}{20,908} = 210\%$

A job or product passing through all four departments would attract departmental overheads at the rates we have just calculated, based on direct labour cost.

An examination of the annual cost analysis will remind us that the rates calculated will have recovered the departmental overheads including the apportioned costs of the service departments, but there are some general factory costs which are not included in the rates. We might agree to absorb these as a rate on direct labour calculated as under:

Cost centres 67/69: General factory $\dfrac{\text{Overheads}}{\text{Direct labour}} = \dfrac{£26,704}{79,608} = 34\%$

The rate so calculated could either be added to the departmental rates to give:

Power press shop	324% + 34% = 358%
Fly press shop	135% + 34% = 169%
Assembly shop	100% + 34% = 134%
Finishing shop	210% + 34% = 244%

Alternatively, it could be shown separately on costs or estimates as a separate 34·% rate on direct labour.

This method of recovering the overheads of factory departments is very popular, because it is relatively easy to compute and apply. Nevertheless, it has some defects, the main one being that overheads are usually not related to direct labour cost but to operation times. This can be illustrated quite simply by the case where male and female operators both work particular machines at different levels of earnings for approximately the same output. Under these circumstances, the female operator would attract less overhead expenses than the male operator. This would not be accurate. The overhead cost per hour of operating a machine is likely to be near enough the same whoever is the operator.

Time rates. Many consider that factory overhead rates based on time are more accurate. Some departments are essentially machine departments, where the rate calculated would be called a machine hour rate, while others are departments of manual operations where the rate calculated would be a direct labour hour rate. One would expect a machine hour rate to be much higher than a labour hour rate because of the incidence in the former of machine running costs.

Example. Cost centre 50: Power press shop. It is estimated that during the course of the year, the press operating hours will total 50,722. Normally, this will cover actual production hours, excluding all down time for set-up, breakdown, and the like. A machine hour rate, or press hour rate, if that sounds more appropriate, would be calculated by dividing the overheads of the department, £76,083, by the press operating hours, 50,722. This would give an overhead rate of £1·50 per press hour. The implication of this is that every job passing through the power press shop would receive an overhead charge calculated by multiplying the operation time by the £1·50 overhead rate per hour.

The time rate method of calculating overhead rates will now be clear. It is normally more difficult to calculate time rates, because operating time information must be available, and in many factories where money piecework methods of remuneration are in use, such information is not recorded. Nevertheless, it can be argued that time rates are likely to be more accurate, mainly because many overhead costs are related to time. For example, one could say that the costs of space—building occupation costs, as these are often called—are essentially annual costs. It would be reasonable to suggest that in a machine department the use of tools, consumables, and power, increase in more or less direct proportion to operating hours. If the time rate method is used, then we do not incur the problem that was mentioned in the previous section when costing the work coming from male and female operators.

In many organizations, cost estimating is simplified by the use of time rates which include both the overhead and the direct labour content of departmental costs. If we take the example of the assembly shop in our annual cost analysis, we would add together direct wages, £28,827, and overheads, £28,651, to give a total of £57,478, which we would then divide by the direct labour hours, £100,000, to give a rate of 57·5p per direct labour hour. The estimated assembly time on any job would be multiplied by this rate to give the appropriate charge to the job both for direct labour and overheads in that department.

Percentage of prime cost. In a very small number of organizations, factory overhead rates are calculated as a percentage of prime cost. If we take the finishing shop as our example of this calculation, the departmental overheads amounting to £43,813 would be expressed as a percentage of the prime cost incurred in that department, £61,922. This would give a rate of 78 %, which would then be applied to every job passing through this department on the basis of its prime cost. The modern view is that this is not a particularly equitable method of absorbing overheads, because so few overheads are related in any way to material costs.

It must be pointed out at this stage that in calculating the time rates and the percentage on prime cost rate, no allowance was made for the general factory overheads, which would presumably still be recovered on the basis of direct labour. Alternatively, some method could be devised to apportion these costs to the individual departments, so that they could then be included in the departmental rates.

Administration Costs

It is usual for the costs of administration to be classified separately, as they are in our annual cost analysis, and also to be absorbed separately in product costs. There are many methods of absorption in use, but the most common are:

1 As a percentage of factory cost.
2 As a percentage of factory conversion costs—that is, factory cost less the cost of direct material input.

Percentage of factory cost. To illustrate this, let us refer back to our cost exercise. On the annual cost analysis, administration costs have been collected under Cost Centre Codes 72 to 75. Adding the costs of these four cost centres together gives a grand total of £30,110. To arrive at a total of factory costs, we have to add figures as follows:

Factory costs	
Power press shop	£207,207
Fly press shop	£62,012
Assembly shop	£220,340
Finishing shop	£105,735
General factory	£26,704
	£621,998

If we now express the administration costs totalling £30,110 as a percentage of the total of factory costs, £621,998, the rate of overhead absorption works out at 4·86%. The implication of the calculation made is that when, in product costing, we have calculated the factory cost of a product on the basis of materials, direct labour, and factory overheads, we would then add to this factory cost 4·86% to recover the costs of administration.

The percentage of factory cost method can be very inequitable, in the same way that the percentage of prime cost method for recovering factory overheads was seen to be inaccurate. A large part of factory cost is often the cost of direct materials: in this particular case, it amounts to £342,577, or 55% of factory cost. This means that a large proportion of the administrative costs is being recovered on the basis of direct materials, and it could well be argued that much of this cost will not be in any way related to material input. A component made out of different materials would attract a different amount of administration costs according to the cost of the material used: this would not necessarily be accurate.

Percentage of factory conversion cost. In this case we are relating the administration costs to factory costs less direct materials, so that the appropriate figures in our example are:

Administration costs		£30,110
Factory conversion cost		
Factory cost	£621,998	
Less direct materials	£342,577	
		£279,421

The percentage rate would then work out at 10·8%. The implication of this calculation is that in costing the company's products, the factory cost would be calculated under the headings of materials, labour, and overheads, and then the costs of administration would be added at the rate of 10·8% on the labour and overheads only.

This is generally thought of as a more equitable method of absorbing administration costs.

Selling and Distribution Costs

In the annual cost analysis these total £74,278, and these costs are frequently recovered as a percentage of the sales value of the product. The annual cost analysis shows total costs of £726,386, so that if we assume a rate of profit of 10% on total costs, the saleable value of the output would be £800,000 approximately, If we related the selling and distribution costs to this turnover figure, it would amount to 9·28%. When costing products, selling and distribution costs could be added to factory and administration costs by taking 9·28% of the product selling price. One could argue that this is not a particularly satisfactory way of absorbing these costs, on the grounds that a selling price is not really a function of cost. One could also ask how these costs would be absorbed in an estimate for a new product which had no selling price; frequently, this is achieved by relating selling and distribution costs to the total of factory and administration cost. In this case, this would give $\dfrac{£74,278}{£652,108} = 11·4\%$.

It must be understood that this has not been an exhaustive treatment of the methods of absorbing overhead expenses. If we recapitulate, normal practice is to classify the overheads of a business into divisions, then into the departments within divisions, and perhaps into cost centres within each department; after that we relate the overheads of each section to what we consider the most appropriate unit of measurement. The search for appropriate units of measurement is a continuous one.

Methods of Product Costing

Costing is appropriate to any type of business, not only to manufacturing businesses. A business engaged in factoring, a departmental store, a repair shop, a municipal undertaking, a transport organization, and many non-commercial units such as hospitals have need of, and make use of, costing. From a costing point of view, the basic difference between one organization and another is the cost unit, that is, the service, job, product, or order which the business renders or makes.

Let us consider the different types of cost unit. If the business is a manufacturing business and produces motor cars, then we will want to know the cost of each model of car. Another manufacturing business may be engaged in heavy constructional engineering work, where each job or contract is different: in this case we will wish to know the cost of each job or contract. As far as manufacturing is concerned, the cost unit depends on the product and the type of manufacture. There are circumstances, such as in jobbing, where each job would be costed separately; on the other hand, if one is engaged in the cooking of biscuits, one would compute a process cost which would enable one to cost biscuits in appropriate amounts or weights. If we move outside manufacturing, the cost units are again different. Take a hospital, where the interesting piece of cost information is the cost per patient/day or per bed/day.

Inevitably, the considerable variation in cost units gives rise to a variation in the method of product costing. Basically the methods are as follows:

1 *Unit costing*, where the organization manufactures only one product. The cost per product can be arrived at by dividing the costs in any period by the output. Here, we do not need to calculate rates of overhead absorption.

2 *Job or contract or batch costing*. Costs are arrived at for each individual works order, which is for a separate product or batch of products for a particular customer. This is particularly appropriate in jobbing engineering or civil engineering. Where a business is engaged in small-batch production, each batch order may be costed as a separate job, and then the order cost is divided by the number in the batch to give a cost per unit.

3 *Operating costing*. Oddly enough, this is the method appropriate to a hospital, but not for the obvious reason. This method is applicable where a service is rendered and global costs must be divided by the amount of the service rendered to give a unit cost. This is true of a hospital, with its bed/day unit of cost, and of a transport undertaking, with its passenger/mile or ton/mile unit.

4 *Process costing*. Particularly appropriate to the manufacture of chemicals or food processing, the implication here is that the product is produced through a series of processes, so that each process has to be costed before the product can be costed. The product cost is arrived at by accumulating a series of process costs.

5 *Operation costing*, of particular use in the manufacture of repetitive parts through a series of operations. In fact, this is the engineering equivalent of the process industries method of costing. If the product passes through a series of operations with costs, scrap, and rejects being incidental at each, then each operation has to be costed before the product can be costed.

Example of product costing. The supervisory manager will be more interested in the costs of his own department, and how they can be controlled and reduced, than in the detailed costs of products. It would be unreasonable to spend too much time on the detail of product costing, but we should examine at least one example.

We have seen an annual cost analysis, which was in fact carried out by the Bluebell Manufacturing Company Limited, which has its factory and warehouse in Walsall, in Staffordshire. The company makes electric fires and a convector heater, along with tubular electric heaters and immersion heaters.

The company was formed in 1933 as a private company, and converted to a public company in 1948 when demand for the company's products necessitated going to the public for additional share capital. Since 1948 it has been registered with the Registrar of Companies, with an authorized capital of £300,000.

There are three directors; one is a working director, who acts as chairman and managing director.

There are four productive departments in the factory—the fly press shop and the power press shop, where pressing is carried out on sheet metal, the finishing department, where a variety of operations is executed, and the assembly shop, where the products are finish-assembled for packing and warehousing. The factory services comprise a toolroom, a maintenance team which looks after the power house, the stores, and a factory administration team including a planner, work study men, and a material controller. There are the usual office departments responsible to the secretary/accountant, a buying department, and a sales division.

Costs are required for three products:

(a) 1 kW electric fire.
(b) 2 kW electric fire.
(c) 2 kW convector heater.

Each of the three products passes through each of the three manufacturing departments and it is relatively easy to establish the prime cost of each product. In fact, the average prime cost has been calculated and is shown below. This prime cost varies according to such factors as the waste of material, the quantity of production rejects, and the rate of output, and so on.

Average Prime Costs of Products

Materials			1 kW fire	2 kW fire	2 kW convector
			p	p	p
M.S. sheet			22·50	27·00	61·22
Expanded metal			—	—	7·50
N.S. wire			7·50	15·00	43·33
Fireclay formers			5·00	10·00	27·50
Switch			—	8·75	8·75
Flex			3·75	3·75	5·00
Sundries			7·50	10·00	58·75
Silvering (outwork)			3·33	4·16	—
			49·58	78·66	212·05

Labour	*Grade*	(p/hr.)	min.	p	min.	p	min.	p
Pressing/fly	F	25·00	2	0·83	3	1·25	6	2·50
Pressing/power	M	37·50	6	3·75	8	5·00	12	7·50
Assembly	F	25·00	10	4·17	15	6·25	30	12·50
Finishing	M	37·50	6	3·75	8	5·00	12	7·50
			24	12·50	34	17·50	60	30·00

Since we have now calculated appropriate overhead rates for each department and division of this company, we will set about completing the costs of the sample three products. How it might work out is shown on the following page.

Thus we can arrive at the costs of the individual products made by the organization, and get some idea of the profit made on each. There is a very considerable difference between *costing* and *estimating*. If the work demonstrated above is carried out before a job is executed or a product is made, then this is estimating. It may be done extremely accurately by persons with very considerable technical skill, but at the best, it is still only an opinion. On the other hand, if the work demonstrated above is carried out after manufacture of the product or a batch of the products, then this is costing, often referred to as actual or historical costing.

Product Costs

	1 kW fire		2 W fikre		2 kW convector	
	min.	p	min.	p	min.	p
Materials (in total)		49·58		78·66		212·05
Labour						
Fly press	2	0·83	3	1·25	6	2·50
Power press	6	3·75	8	5·00	12	7·50
Assembly	10	4·17	15	6·25	30	12·50
Finishing	6	3·75	8	5·00	12	7·50
	24	12·50	34	17·50	60	30·00
Departmental overheads						
Fly press 135% of D.L.		1·12		1·69		3·38
Power press 324% of D.L.		12·15		16·20		24·30
Assembly 100% of D.L.		4·17		6·25		12·50
Finishing 210% of D.L.		7·88		10·50		15·75
		25·32		34·64		55·93
General Factory overheads						
34% of D.L.		4·25		5·95		10·20
		91·65		136·75		308·18
Administration overheads						
10·8% of factory conversion cost		9·90		14·77		33·28
		101·55		151·52		341·46
Selling and distribution overheads						
11·4% of factory and admin. cost		11·57		17·27		38·93
		113·12		168·79		380·39
Total costs		£1·13		1·69		3·80
Selling prices		£1·25		1·88		4·00
Profit		£0·12		0·19		0·20

SUMMARY

1 *Where does the costing function fit into the organization?*

The costing function is a part of the accounting division, but this should not preclude co-operation with all levels of management throughout the business.

2 *What is the role of the supervisory manager in costing?*

The supervisory manager is in charge of a department which incurs cost, so that he has a cost responsibility—namely, to keep costs within bounds, to eliminate or reduce costs. He should know his costs.

3 *How are costs analysed?*

(a) Into materials, wages and expenses, (b) into direct and indirect, (c) into divisions, departments, and cost centres within departments.

4 *What is meant by prime cost?*

The sum of *direct materials*, *direct wages*, and *direct expenses*.

5 *What are overheads?*

These are *indirect materials*, *indirect wages*, and *indirect expenses*.

6 *What is the difference between cost allocation and cost apportionment?*

If cost can be identified with a department and charged directly to it, then the cost is said to be *allocated*, but if a cost has to be split between departments on some basis, then it is said to have been *apportioned*.

7 *Of what use is cost analysis?*

It tells us what our costs are and which are the most significant. It gives us the detailed knowledge of costs necessary for cost control. It enables us to calculate cost rates, which will help in cost estimating and in the computation of product costs.

8 *What is meant by absorption of overhead costs?*

Their recovery in the costs of products.

9 *What are the basic difficulties of overhead cost absorption?*

They are (1) determination of the level of overhead expenditure which is relevant, and (2) determination of the method of absorption to be used.

10 *What are the main methods of absorbing factory overheads?*

(1) As a percentage of direct labour, (2) as a rate per machine or labour hour, (3) as a percentage of prime cost.

11 *How would you calculate a percentage of direct labour rate?*

By expressing the overheads of the department as a percentage of the direct labour in that department.

12 *Why not a 'blanket rate' for the factory as a whole?*

This would not be accurate. There are many departments, with a different incidence of cost in each, so that individual departmental rates are called for.

13 *What are the main methods of absorbing administration overheads?*

As a percentage of factory cost, or as a percentage of factory conversion cost.

14 *How would you absorb selling and distribution costs?*

Either as a percentage of the sales price or of factory plus administration costs.

15 *What is meant by a cost unit?*

The product, job, or order which is made by the business, and for which we require to know the cost.

16 *Why do we talk of different methods of costing?*

Because there are different ways of making products and rendering services, and the method of costing must vary according to the method used.

17 *What is the difference between costing and estimating?*

Whereas estimating is the predetermination of costs, costing is the determination of actual costs after the event.

CHAPTER 9 | Cost Characteristics and Behaviour

Every supervisory manager is aware of the human problems in running a department. In discussing the management job so far we have emphasized planning and controlling in terms of systems, not people. But a business organization is only as good as its personnel, and people have characteristics and are variable in their behaviour.

The good supervisory manager finds and recognizes the characteristics of the individuals working for him, and knows how to bring out the best in them. He can anticipate the behaviour of individuals, and plan and control accordingly. He will adjust his methods of supervision according to the individual foibles and peculiarities of each operator in his section.

This human problem is extremely significant in achieving satisfactory productivity. If high productivity implies the best possible use of all resources, then we must not forget human resources. On the other hand, high productivity tends to be reflected in a low cost per unit of output.

Cost Characteristics
Costs, like human beings, have characteristics and patterns of behaviour. To illustrate this simply, the cost of the fuel needed to raise steam for factory heating will tend to increase in winter, because the outside temperature decreases at this time of year. In other words, there is a pattern to factory heating costs. To illustrate this in another way, the supervisory manager of the department is paid a salary, which is a cost that tends to remain relatively fixed. (If you are that supervisory manager, you will probably be hoping that it does not remain fixed for too long!) There are other costs which do not have this fixed characteristic. Take the consumption of tools in your own department: these costs probably vary from week to week. Why do they vary? Factors which will cause variation include a change in the throughput of the department, the advent of a learner-operator who is wrecking the tools at the moment, the supervisory manager's own ability to keep in check a piecework operator who tends to burn tools up, and many other reasons. Thus some costs are much more fixed than others. And then there is the matter of who controls costs and whose is the responsibility for control. Obviously the supervisory manager cannot control costs which are authorized and influenced by top management—such as

consultancy fees—but he can take action about costs which arise in his own department and which he influences.

To sum up, the basic characteristics of cost are those of controllability, normality, and variability.

Controllability. The questions here are: Who controls cost? Whose responsibility is it to exercise control? Where should this responsibility be located? If costs are to be controlled, then the control points must be established and there must be a person responsible for each control point. This is logical enough, but it is surprising how often the basic principle is ignored in practice. Supervisory managers are often asked why certain costs have been allowed to get out of hand, ignoring the fact that control cannot in this particular case be exercised by the departmental supervisor. The characteristic of controllability of each item of cost must be observed and acted upon.

Normality. In Chapter 8 we examined an annual cost analysis, which gave us a knowledge of costs and which had certain uses. But did this historical cost information tell us the extent to which costs incurred in that period were normal or abnormal? Any statement of historical figures may be based on an accounting period in which certain occurrences can be construed as abnormal. Such abnormalities could include:

1 The normal number of working days were not worked in this particular period because of flood damage.
2 The flood damage would have given rise to certain exceptional costs.
3 Several large contracts from one customer made possible much longer production runs than normal, making a difference in the incidence of set-up time, and therefore the relationship between overhead and operating hours.
4 An abnormal cost came up in the period due to a redundancy, in respect of which some considerable redundancy payments were made.

It is important to get some idea of the extent of normal and abnormal costs in historical statements before using them as the base for future cost budgets. In spite of the rather dogmatic attitude we took in the previous chapter over calculating overhead rates, we must take normality into consideration before finally deciding what rates to use in estimating and product costing.

Variability. Putting it simply, some costs are fixed and some are variable. A fixed cost is one which tends to remain constant whatever the level of production or sales, whatever the throughput, whatever the activity. A variable cost is one which tends to vary more or less directly with output or sales. In practice, there will be some costs which are neither fixed nor variable, but a mixture of both. Let us illustrate all of these.

Building occupation costs, rent, rates, depreciation of buildings, and the heating of premises—these are costs which tend to remain fixed whatever the activity in the factory. True, the cost of heating will be different in winter and in summer, but this is not variability in the costing sense. Perhaps the best example of a variable cost is direct material. If it takes 5p worth of material to make one component, it will take 50p worth of material to make ten components. In other words, the cost is strictly variable, moving directly in sympathy with output. There are variable overheads, some of which the departmental supervisor has responsibility for controlling. Tools and consumables have already been mentioned; power cost and the cost of indirect labour might also be included.

The characteristic of variability is most important. One does not have an accurate conception of costs without knowledge of the extent to which costs vary, and with what. It is impossible to budget costs at different levels of production without this knowledge, and that amounts to saying that we cannot produce a profit plan without this knowledge.

Relationship of Costs to Volume

How much does it cost you to run your motor car? One person may say £220 per year, another 4p per mile. Either is wrong. This is because some of the costs of running a motor car are fixed, being incurred on an annual or period basis, whereas others vary more or less directly with the number of miles run.

Let us illustrate this with some figures. The fixed costs might be:

Depreciation of the vehicle	£100	per annum
Insurance	£30	per annum
Road fund tax	£17·5	per annum
Garaging	£22·5	per annum
	£170	per annum

These costs will be incurred irrespective of the number of miles run. On the other hand, the following costs are variable:

Petrol and Oil. During the year
  you travelled 8,500 miles,
  and you averaged 28 miles
  per gallon. You bought the
  best petrol, and you used a
  few pints of oil as well.   £85   for the year

Repairs, maintenance, replacements of tyres, batteries,
  and the like. On average: £42·5 per annum
                                     ————
                                     £127·5 for a year when 8,500
                                     =====   miles were covered

These costs can be thought of in terms of a cost per mile. The
consumption of petrol and oil increases with the mileage run. More
miles on the clock means miles nearer to the next service, the
replacement of a tyre, etc. Harking back to our previous comments
about cost characteristics and behaviour, let us remember that oil
consumption can be as much a function of engine efficiency and age
as of mileage, demonstrating once more how important it is to have
knowledge of cost characteristics. If we calculate the variable costs
as a cost per mile, they work out at $\dfrac{£127·5}{8,500} = 1\tfrac{1}{2}$p per mile. Now
we are in a position to say in answer to the original question that
our costs for running a motor car come out at £170 per annum plus
1½p per mile, and this is the accurate way to express costs.

If the costs must be expressed in terms of an overall total cost,
then we must be told upon what mileage this total cost is to be based.
In the example given, the 8,500 miles run have cost £170 of fixed
costs, and £127·5 of variable costs, giving a total cost of £297·5.
But this total cost is only applicable   8,500 miles run in 1 calendar
year. The total cost per mile would be $\dfrac{£297·5}{8,500} = 3\tfrac{1}{2}$p per mile, but
again this is only the total cost per mile if we run 8,500 miles in 1
calendar year. We see that total costs depend upon activity, or what
in industry we often call volume, or the volume of throughput.
Because some costs are fixed and some are variable, the ultimate cost
per unit will vary according to the level of activity at which we are
operating, and in the same way the total of operating costs will
depend upon the total volume.

We will now put the cost of operating our car on to a graph, so
that we can read off the total cost at several different mileages per

annum. This graph will then show us what is often called the cost structure (Fig. 6).

From Fig. 6, we can read off the total cost at any number of miles per annum. For example, at 2,000 miles the costs total £200, or 10p per mile. At 4,000 miles costs total £230, or 5·75p per mile. On the other hand, if we jump to a mileage of 10,000 per annum, the total costs are £320, which is 3·20p per mile.

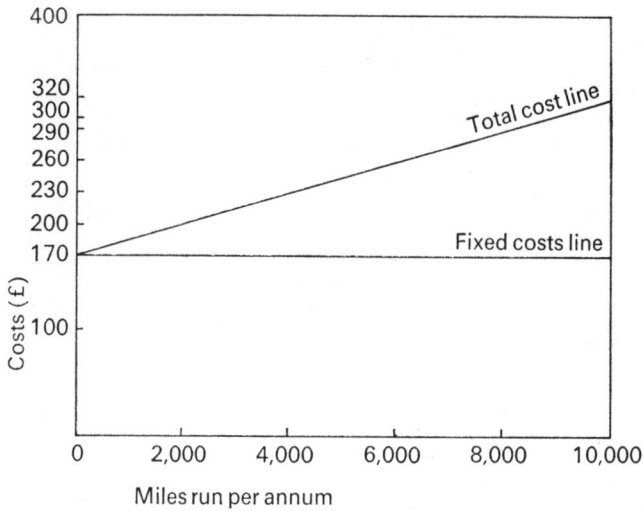

FIG. 6. *Cost structure*

This same structure applies in a manufacturing business or any other sort of commercial organization. The implication of this is that unit costs will tend to be higher when the business is operating at a low volume, and lower when the business is operating at a higher volume. As noted previously, the characteristic of variability is significant in budgeting. Planning implies a pre-determination of the volume of activity at which the business will be running, and reliable estimates of what the costs will be at that volume of activity. The relationship of costs to volume is extremely important, as will be evident when we bring in the factor of sales income.

Break-even Analysis

So far we have been talking costs. These costs will have been used to make products or provide services, for which we will receive a sales income. One factor of real significance when considering the matter of profit is the factor of sales price. Let us go back to our example of the motor car. As a supervisory manager, you probably use your car to get to the factory or office, to get home again, and to do some pleasure motoring. Let us imagine that you are using your motor car for the purpose of making a living, that is, as a taxi: we will assume that the cost structure is exactly the same as previously indicated, that is, fixed costs at £170 per annum and variable costs

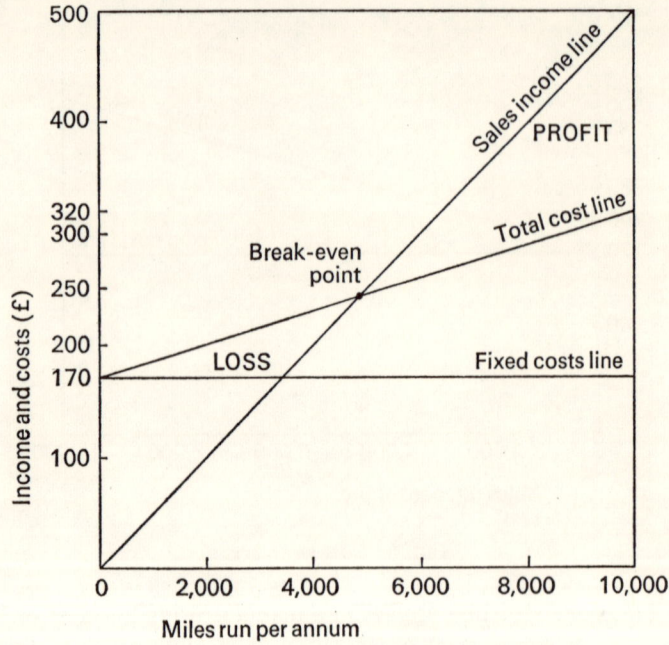

FIG. 7. *Income and costs related to mileage*

at 1½p per mile. How will we fix a selling price for the use of your taxi?

Presumably the selling price will be a rate per mile, and this rate per mile might well be fixed by some local association of taxi drivers. In other words, you probably would not have the opportunity of basing your selling price on your own costs: this is not unusual. All businesses are bound and restricted by competition. Let us think of a selling price of 5p per mile. Now we could extend our graph (see Fig. 7). The previous graph showed only the fixed costs and the total costs at different levels of activity: the new one shows us also the sales income at different mileages, and the profit or loss which we would make at different 'volumes'.

First, note that there is a point on the graph at which the total cost line and the sales line intersect. This is the break-even point, the point at which we make neither profit nor loss. On our graph this point occurs at an income figure of £243. Below this point we are making losses: for example, at 4,000 miles per annum our sales income is £200, our costs are £230, so that the loss is £30 per annum. On the other hand, above this point we are making profits: for example, at 10,000 miles sales income totals £500, costs are £320, so that we make a profit in the year of £180.

This graph is a break-even graph. If we can obtain reasonably accurate information on the cost structure of a business we can construct a graph of this kind. The main requirement is that we should know which of our costs are fixed and which are variable. The main advantage that we get from the break-even graph is our knowledge of profits and losses at different levels of activity. In a practical situation, we find that costs are not simply fixed or variable, but that some costs tend to be what we call semi-fixed and semi-variable. As a good example of this latter, consider fuel for furnace heating: a certain amount of fuel has to be used merely to keep the temperature of the furnace at normal; then extra consumption tends to vary directly with the throughput of the furnace. To illustrate the use of the break-even graph as it might be applied to a manufacturing business, we give details of a manufacturing situation and the sales and cost structure, which is then expressed in the form of a break-even graph which we will interpret.

Example. The Sutton Manufacturing Co. Ltd produces a range of standard products for which the variable costs average 60% of the sales. Fixed costs total some £200,000 per annum, but in addition there are semi-fixed costs which move as follows:

At 10% use of capacity, they total £20,000 per annum
At 30% use of capacity, they total £30,000 per annum
At 50% use of capacity, they total £40,000 per annum
At 70% use of capacity, they total £50,000 per annum

Sales income can be reckoned to be directly variable with the use of capacity, and would be approximately £1 million per annum at 100% capacity.

The graph expresses the same data in more meaningful form. It provides a picture of the profits and losses at different amounts of sales and different levels of capacity utilization. The break-even point is in the region of 61% use of capacity, or sales at the rate of £610,000 per annum. Clearly, at 70% use of capacity there is a

profit of approximately £30,000 per annum. We can prove this
figure from the data given, as follows:

Sales at 70% use of capacity		£700,000
Costs		
Variable costs, 60% of Sales	£420,000	
Semi-fixed costs	£50,000	
Fixed costs	£200,000	
	——————	£670,000
	Profit	£30,000

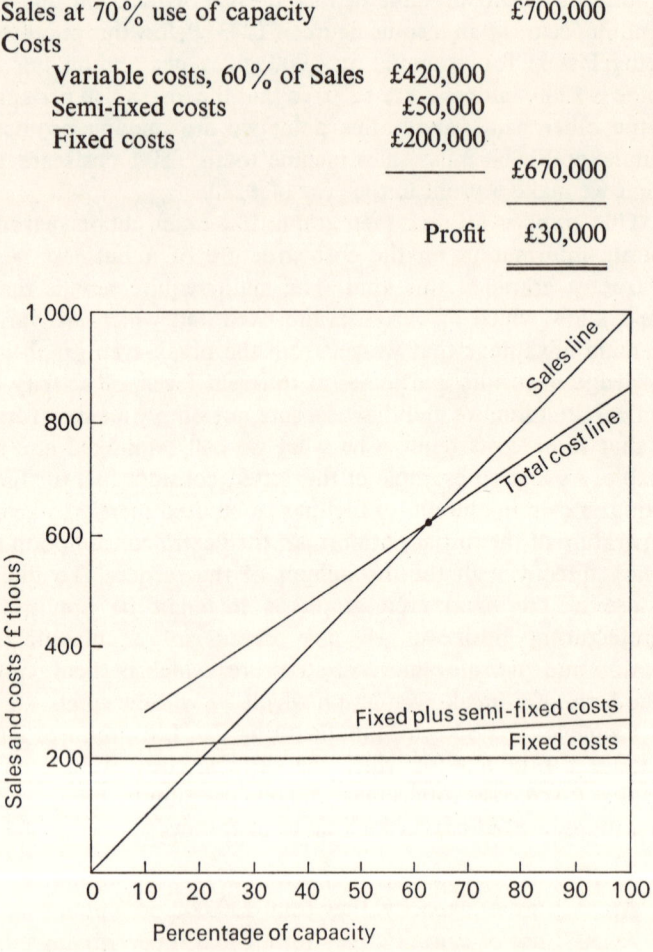

FIG. 8. *Break-even graph*

This example introduces variable costs as a percentage of sales.
This is reasonable, since if variable costs vary directly with sales,
then there is a constant relationship between the two factors.
However, this relationship is not likely to remain constant for a
business in which there is a considerable mix of products.

What are the variable costs? This depends upon the organization,
the products, and the methods of manufacture. In many organizations,

the prime costs can all be regarded as variable costs, but so can some of the overhead expenses—in particular, the costs of tools and consumables, indirect labour, and power. It is reasonable to assume a close relationship between the variable costs and the selling price for each product, so that whether there is a constant relationship overall depends on the extent to which there are changes in the mix of production and sales. This can be illustrated simply. In the case of the Sutton Manufacturing Co. Ltd the variable costs are said to average 60% of sales. But it could be that the manufactures comprise two separate groups of products, one of which shows a 50% relationship of variable costs to sales, the other of which shows a 70% relationship. When the sales of the two product groups are equal, then the relationship will be 60%, but not otherwise. A change in the mix of production and sales will, in practice, bring a change in the relationship between variable costs and sales.

Marginal Costing

Marginal cost is variable cost or, to put it another way, the cost of an additional unit of output. If you make one more unit of production, how much will it cost? An additional increment of output will bring an additional increment of cost. What will this incremental cost comprise? Certainly, we shall require an additional unit of material and an additional increment of labour cost, with an additional unit of all those overheads which associate themselves with the operations to be performed, such as tools, consumables, and power. So the marginal cost is usually the prime cost plus variable overheads. We have not really advanced much on what we said before when talking of fixed and variable costs, but we are now emphasizing that a product will have a marginal cost. We can go on to argue that it does not really have a total cost unless we are prepared to carry out some arbitrary apportionments of cost.

When we compute the total cost of a product, we normally do so by arriving separately at the prime cost elements of direct materials, direct labour, and direct expense, and then we add the various classes of overhead expenses according to agreed formulae. We may be enlightened in our methods of absorbing overheads: for instance, we may use separate cost centre rates for factory overheads. The calculation of these cost centre rates has involved us in the apportionment of very many items of overheads, predominantly the fixed overhead items. For example, we have apportioned building occupation costs, which are essentially fixed on the basis of floor area, and this is of necessity arbitrary. The managing director's salary, another fixed cost item, will presumably have been included in administration overheads, and recovered in relation to the conversion cost of each product. In other words, the total cost of a product is not what it would cost to produce one more unit, because one more unit of output would not be likely to increase building occupation costs or the managing director's salary. The other way of looking at this is to say that since many of the overhead items are fixed and will have to be paid whether production is at 50% or 90% level of activity, there is no point in apportioning these costs in an arbitrary manner to the individual products, but to treat them as a pool of expense to be met by all products in total.

Let us illustrate this with figures. Suppose that we are making a product for which the selling price is £1·00 per unit, and the cost structure has been calculated as follows:

Direct materials	50p
Direct labour	10p
Overheads (absorbed at the rate of 250% on direct labour)	25p
	85p

In these circumstances we could say that the product is making a profit of 15p per unit. On the other hand, we know that the overheads contain some elements which are fixed and some which are variable, so that the rate of 250% on direct labour would only be true for a particular level of activity. If the level of activity in the company drops far enough, an overhead rate applied to direct labour as shown might make the product show a loss rather than a profit. In other words, a product does not really have a total cost, and does not really make a profit. If we must calculate a total cost and a profit then we have to base it on a particular level of activity, and we must involve ourselves in fixed cost apportionments.

However, part of the cost of a product will remain relatively constant no matter what the level of activity—this is the variable or marginal cost. If we calculate this and deduct it from the selling price of the product, then we know what contribution the product makes towards this pool of fixed expenses. Taking the product for which the selling price was £1·00 per unit, the variable or marginal cost might be:

Direct materials	50p
Direct labour (12 minutes)	10p
Variable overheads (absorbed at the rate of 62½p per hour)	12½p
	72½p

If we now deduct the marginal cost from the selling price, we arrive at the contribution made by the product. In this example, the product makes a contribution of 27½p per unit, which we arrive at by subtracting the marginal cost from the selling price. What does this mean? It does not mean that the product makes a profit of 27½p per unit, but that after all the variable costs of producing and selling it have been met, there is still 27½p per unit left to contribute to the fixed expenses of running the business. Further, if we make a sufficient number of units, the contribution will be big enough in total to meet the fixed expense bill, and leave us with a margin of profit.

This is an important concept in costing and profit making. From Fig. 8 we see that above the break-even point, when all the fixed costs have been met, all contribution is net profit. Once again we realize that a total cost of a product can only be calculated at a particular level of activity. At any other level of activity, unit total cost would be different. It may be more valuable for an organization to look at its costs from a marginal costing viewpoint, because the technique of marginal costing may produce more reliable information for decision making—for example, in determining the profitability of products.

Profitability of Products

An organization may be tempted to calculate the relative profitability of its products by deducting total cost from selling price to reveal a net profit figure. It may then relate the net profit made by each product to the total cost, or to the selling price, to get a measure of profitability. Our look at marginal costing should suggest to us a new, more reliable way of calculating product profitability.

Below is an example of a statement of product profitability based on the total cost approach.

Product	Sales units	Sales value £	Total cost £	Net profit £
A	1,000	1,000	900	100
B	1,000	2,000	1,600	400
C	1,000	3,000	3,100	100 loss
		£6,000	£5,600	£400

The impression given by this statement is that Product A is profitable, making a margin of 10% of selling price, Product B is even more profitable, making a margin amounting to 20% of selling price, while Product C is unprofitable. Now in computing the total costs of each of the products, certain expenses, very largely the fixed expenses, have been apportioned to the products on an arbitrary basis. If we eliminated these fixed expenses from the product cost calculations, the statement might look like this:

Product	Sales units	Sales value £	Marginal cost £	Contri- bution £	Fixed costs £	Net profit £
A	1,000	1,000	810	190	—	—
B	1,000	2,000	1,440	560	—	—
C	1,000	3,000	2,790	210	—	—
		£6,000	£5,040	£960	£560	£400

All we have done in the above statement is to remove the fixed costs from the product costs and show them as a separate total which we have deducted from the total of the contributions coming from the products. Now the picture of product profitability looks somewhat different. Whereas in the original statement Product C was seen to be unprofitable, we now know that it does at least make some contribution towards the fixed expenses of the business. From a look at the first statement, we might have been tempted to suggest that Product C should be eliminated from the catalogue, but our marginal cost statement makes it clear that if we did this, we would lose the contribution of £210, which would mean a loss of profit of the same amount, unless of course, we could use the facilities which had been made idle by the elimination of Product C to better advantage.

Conclusion

How do cost characteristics and, in particular, cost variability affect the supervisory manager? They affect him in two main ways.

First, the ability to make profit depends to a considerable extent upon volume. The break-even graphs revealed that profit is higher at higher volumes of output for two reasons:

1 If one is making profit-making products, then the more one sells the more will be the profit.

2 Some costs are fixed no matter what the level of output; therefore, increases in activity will bring more than proportionate increases in profit.

The supervisory manager influences the factor of volume, and has responsibilities in this connection. The throughput of the department rests to a great extent upon his ability.

Second, the amount of profit we make is dependent upon the level of our variable costs, and many of these are controllable by the departmental supervisor. The costs of direct materials, direct labour, and variable overheads can be influenced and controlled by him. The volume of profit in a business depends to a large extent on the ability of individual supervisory managers to control these costs.

SUMMARY

1 *What do we mean when we say that costs have characteristics and patterns of behaviour?*

We mean that some costs are controllable while others are not, some costs are normal or recurring, others are abnormal, some costs are fixed while others are variable.

2 *Why is the characteristic of variability important?*

Without knowledge of the extent to which costs vary, there can be no accurate conception of costs, and it would be impossible to budget them at different levels of production. This means that we could not produce our profit plan.

3 *What is the relationship of costs to volume?*

Some costs increase with an increase in volume, while others remain fixed. As a result, unit cost tends to decrease with an increase in volume, and increase with lower volume.

4 *What is a break-even graph?*

It is a graph which shows the cost structure of a business in terms of fixed and variable costs and compares these costs with the sales income, showing profits and losses at different levels of activity.

5 *What is the break-even point?*

This is the point at which sales income and total costs equate, above which the business makes a profit, below which the business makes a loss.

6 *What are variable costs?*

These are the costs which vary directly with output or sales. Examples are the direct materials, the direct labour, the direct expenses, and certain overhead expenses such as tools and consumables, indirect labour and power.

7 *Which are the fixed costs?*

These are the costs which tend to remain constant whatever the level of output or sales. Such costs are depreciation, salaries, building occupation costs, rent, rates, and most administrative expenses.

8 *What is the marginal cost of a product?*

This is the variable cost which can be attributed to a product—again, the direct materials, direct labour, and direct expenses, plus the variable overheads.

9 *What do we mean by contribution?*

The difference between the marginal cost of a product and its selling price.

10 *From a marginal cost point of view, when do we make profit?*

When contributions from products exceed the fixed expenses of the business.

11 *What are the lessons for the supervisory manager?*

He affects the factor of volume; the throughput of the department rests to a great extent upon his ability. In addition, much of the variable cost is controlled by him.

CHAPTER 10

Standards and Flexible Budgets for Control

Problem of Control

In Chapter 7, the job of management was divided into three main areas: (1) planning, (2) operating or taking action, and (3) measuring and evaluating performance. The term 'control' is often used to cover areas (2) and (3).

We have seen that cost data can be interesting and useful. However, this information does not itself control costs. Costs can only be controlled by people. Indeed, management cannot control costs in the physical sense; what management can do is to attempt to control the actions of those people who are responsible for incurring costs. The problem is therefore mainly concerned with people, and the way in which they approach their jobs. In this chapter we shall examine the kinds of information which are likely to be useful in controlling the actions of people who incur costs.

A foreman in a machine shop is solely responsible for few costs. The amount of labour required for a given output may be specified by the production engineer; the rate of pay of labour will be negotiated by the personnel manager; the number of units to be produced will be determined by the production controller. However, he has a significant influence over the level of a number of costs which are incurred in his department—for instance, the amount of 'lost time' or 'non-productive' time, and the amount of raw material which is scrapped. Although not solely responsible for all overhead expenditure, he will be able to exercise a considerable effect on the level of some of these costs—for example, tools and consumables.

This line of argument can be extended to the job of any supervisory manager. Indeed, a most important part of his job is to determine those costs over which he can exercise a significant influence. The role of the accountant is to give help in determining these costs and thereafter to supply information covering these costs.

What control information does the manager require?

1 The actual level of those costs over which he can exercise a significant influence.
2 To evaluate this information, a statement showing what these costs should have been.

3 As further help in the process of evaluation, a statement highlighting and analysing the difference between the actual level of costs and what these costs should have been.

Need for Standards

Let us assume that the labour bill in a machine shop is £500. What can we say about the performance of the foreman in controlling costs? Very little at the moment; we have no means of judging whether the labour costs should have been £400 or £600. What we need are standards, or a basis of comparison that will tell us what the performance should have been under the conditions existing at the time.

The responsibility for setting such standards rests with the individual manager. Although some companies have work study departments or organization and methods departments, which specialize in setting standards, it is an essential part of the job of any manager to set goals or yardsticks for those costs over which he can exercise a significant influence. The specialist departments are available to give assistance to the line manager, but the ultimate responsibility rests with the manager himself.

We saw in Chapter 8 that forecasts and plans are made on the assumption that a high level of efficiency will be attained. This means that in drawing up plans, managers must determine what is meant by a high level of efficiency. Thus the setting of standards or yardsticks is an essential step in the formulation of worth-while plans, and also a vital factor in the evaluation of the efforts to carry out these plans.

A useful starting point in the setting of standards is the study of past cost behaviour. Such study allows the classification of costs as fixed, variable, or semi-variable. However, the level of efficiency included in a budget should not merely be an extension of past experience. Past costs may have involved inefficiencies, and in addition it is possible that changes in methods or equipment may affect the level of costs in the future. The standards should ideally be set after a careful analysis of the job, the methods which are used, and the efficiency of performance. In practice, detailed targets are often established for two major elements of cost, *direct labour* and *direct materials*. These targets are used in the technique of standard costing. All other costs are usually controlled with the help of departmental overhead budgets.

Control of Direct Labour

A standard labour cost is a predetermined cost based on an assessment of the operations, machines, and type of labour necessary to produce a product efficiently, and the time taken to do so. A rate of pay is related to this. Note that a number of managers contribute to the establishment of a standard labour cost. In accordance with the design issued by the design engineer, the production engineer will specify the operational layout which will show the operations, the machines, and the type of layout to be used. The work study engineer will specify the time to be taken when the job is performed according to the operation layout. The personnel manager will be responsible for wage administration. In operating a standard cost system, the accountant will co-ordinate the standards already set by managers. The reports issued by the accountant will show how well the company is adhering to the standards of performance detailed by these managers. Often the job of establishing standards for labour is carried out as part of the system of wages payment, and the information which is already available for that purpose can be used in dealing with the problem of control.

Example. In a general machine shop standard labour cards might be issued for each operation showing the standard time allowed and the rate of pay. If time in excess of the standard needed to be worked, this would be authorized by the foreman, after the reasons had been given and any necessary corrective action had been taken. This excess cost would be coded to the cost centre where it had been incurred, and summarized at the end of the week at the standard rate of pay in the departmental labour efficiency report.

A simple report for summarizing the information on direct labour is given overleaf, and may be adapted to meet specific circumstances.

In Part A, the total actual hours are shown for each operator. The total hours during which the operator was employed in productive work are also shown, together with the standard hours which were produced during that productive time. Two measures of efficiency have been calculated. The first, which we can call the measured work performance ratio, or efficiency ratio, compares actual and standard performance for a certain quantity of work. The second, which we can call attendance time performance ratio, or productivity ratio, shows how efficient an operator has been over a period of time.

Both measures are a guide to the efficiency which has been

achieved, but more information is necessary to show why actual performance varied from standard.

Departmental Labour Efficiency Report

Week ending 29th September

Part A. Operator Efficiency

Cost centre	Operator, name	Clock no.	Total actual hours 1	Total productive hours 2	Standard hours produced 3	Efficiency % 3/2	Productivity % 3/1	Non-productive time 1–2	Analysis reasons
PP1	J. Brown	87	50	40	32	80	64	10	Waiting for tools
PP1	B. Adams	74	45	40	42	105	93	5	Waiting instructions
FP1	C. Jones	92	48	42	42	100	87	6	Maintenance
FP1	J. Back	84	46	42	46	109	100	4	Waiting for work
	Etc.								
	Total		1020	912	874	96	86	108	

Part B. Analysis of the Cost of Non-productive Time and Other Excess Costs

Rate variance arising from		Use variance arising from		
	£		Hrs	£
Overtime	20	Waiting for work	21	11
Shift allowance	10	Waiting for instructions	6	3
Over-rated labour	16	Waiting for material	18	9
Make-up and awards	12	Waiting for setters	14	7
		Training	15	8
		Scrap	11	5
		Rectification	11	5
		Alternative methods	12	6
Total	58	Total	108	54

This requirement is fulfilled in Part B, which gives an analysis of the cost of non-productive time and other excess costs which have been incurred. The difference between standard costs and actual costs is first separated into rate or price variances and then into use or quantity variances. The cost of various excesses is then given under each heading. A good supervisory manager will be aware of the occurrence of these excesses and will already be working to correct the situation. However, it is extremely useful for him to see where the cost leaks are occurring and how much they are costing the company.

Control of Raw Material

A standard material cost is an estimated cost, based on a technical specification of the materials, making due allowance for reasonable scrap and waste, and priced at the expected price level over a reasonable period—for example, 1 year.

As in the case of the standard labour cost, a number of managers contribute to the establishment of a standard material cost. The design engineer, in addition to preparing the product design, will specify the materials to be used in its manufacture. The production engineer will specify the operation layout, and also the amount of material which should be used if the layout is adhered to. The buying office will supply details of the expected price levels. Armed with this information, the accountant has the straightforward task of compiling the raw material standard cost, which has built into it the standards of performance specified by a number of managers. The reports issued by the accountant will show to what extent these standards are achieved in practice, and the excess costs which are incurred in departing from the established standards.

A simple example of this in the case of the general machine shop would be provided by the issue of the standard amount of material to complete a job. If material is required in excess of the standard, this would be authorized by the foreman after the reasons had been stated, and any necessary corrective action had been taken. This excess cost would be coded to the cost centre where it had been incurred, and summarized at the end of the week at the standard price in the departmental material efficiency report.

The material costs which are in excess of the standard costs are shown against each operator. The reason for this excess arising from usage is analysed under six main headings.

A good foreman would be aware of these losses but once again it is valuable for foremen and supervisory managers to see where material cost excesses are occurring and what is their cost to the company.

The excess cost arising from the difference between the standard price of material and the actual price has not been shown on the departmental report, since the supervisory manager is not able to exercise a significant influence over this cost. The price variance is more likely to be a reflection on the performance of the buying department than on the efforts of the manufacturing department. If factory accounts were compiled, it would be necessary to show the factory manager the extent of the losses incurred through material

Departmental Material Efficiency Report

Cost centre	Operator, name	Clock no.	Use variance		Analysis					
			Physical lbs	£	Scrap operator	Waste excess	Faulty material	Faulty M/c	Alternative Specification	Others
PP1	J. Brown	87	860	16	10	6				
PP1	B. Adams	74	270	5	1	2	2			
FP1	C. Jones	92	340	6	2			4		
FP1	J. Back	84	980	18	6	4			8	
	Etc.									
	Total		10,100	187	62	47	23	24	12	19

price variances. The trend of material prices cannot be foreseen with the same accuracy as changes in labour rates. We have assumed that negotiated changes in labour rate variances which are shown on the labour efficiency report are, therefore, costs over which the foreman has some control.

Control of Overheads

In dealing with the control of direct labour and direct material the emphasis has been on the necessity of fixing responsibility, of setting standards, and of measuring performance against the standards.

This basic approach is also applicable when dealing with the control of overhead expenses. However, detailed standards are often more difficult to establish in this area, and also the level of expense for individual items may not justify elaborate control procedures. The usual way of controlling overhead costs is by the use of flexible budgets. The main feature of these budgets is that they provide bases of comparison for different levels of volume.

Let us compare a fixed budget with a flexible budget. We will assume that the planned level of activity for the next week in the general machine shop is 10,000 units. The following is the budgeted level of overheads which might be applicable to that level of output.

General Machining Department
Fixed Budget—Overheads
Week ending 29th September

Units to be produced	10,000
Indirect labour	£500
Tools	£200
Oils	£100
Consumables	£100
Maintenance	£100
	£1,000

At the end of the week, the units produced were 9,000. Machine breakdowns and shortage of materials had restricted production.

Using the fixed budget approach the overhead efficiency report would be as follows:

General Machining Department
Overhead Efficiency Report
Fixed budget. Week ending 29th September

	Budget	Actual	Variance	
Units produced	10,000	9,000	1,000	Unfavourable
Indirect labour	£500	£470	£30	Favourable
Tools	£200	£190	£10	Favourable
Oils	£100	£100	—	
Consumables	£100	£90	£10	Favourable
Maintenance	£100	£85	£15	Favourable
	£1,000	£935	£65	

In Chapter 7, we saw that the supervisory manager was responsible for performance and cost. The above statement reports on performance or output, but is misleading on cost. The fixed budget report indicates that the supervisory manager has performed satisfactorily in his control of overhead costs. However, in order to judge this, we need to set against actual overhead costs not the target costs for an output of 10,000 units, but the budgeted overhead costs for the actual output of 9,000 units. The flexible budget approach gives us this information, since in this method the budget is tailored to any level of activity. Assuming that the behaviour of costs is strictly variable, the flexible budget report is as follows:

General Machining Department
Overhead Efficiency Report
Flexible budget. Week ending 29th September

Budgeted output	10,000	Activity	100%
Units produced	9,000	Activity	90%

	Budget at 100% activity	Budget at 90% activity	Actual	Variance	
Indirect labour	£500	£450	£470	£20	Unfavourable
Tools	£200	£180	£190	£10	Unfavourable
Oils	£100	£90	£100	£10	Unfavourable
Consumables	£100	£90	£90	—	
Maintenance	£100	£90	£85	£5	Favourable
	£1,000	£900	£935	£35	Unfavourable

Note that in this case the variances show a more unfavourable performance under the flexible budget system compared with the fixed budget system. Unfavourable variances are not always signs of inefficiency on the part of the supervisory manager. However, from the point of view of the company, unfavourable variances do represent cost leaks which reduce the profit available to the company. The flexible budget approach of tailoring the budgeted costs to the actual level of activity provides a useful tool which can be used to control overhead costs at a high level of efficiency.

We assumed in our example that the behaviour of the overhead costs was strictly variable. In practice the behaviour of overhead costs is likely to be a mixture of fixed and variable. This means that cost studies will be required which will assess the degree of variability at different levels of activity. This measure of cost variability of each item of overhead expenditure will then be used to calculate the flexible overhead budget.

Control of Clerical Work
The preceding examples have been concerned with a general machine shop. However, the basic principles of control apply just

Control Office Statement

Department: General Sales Office · *Supervisor:* Mr W. Smith

Workload	Time each (hours)	Average workload		Actual workload	
		Quantity	Total hours	Quantity	Total hours
Credit sales	0·1216	13,036	1,585	13,140	1,597
Credit repairs	0·5050	624	315	794	401
Cash sales	0·0583	905	53	1,247	73
Cash repairs	0·3083	216	66	304	94
Sales counter transactions	0·1021	2,342	239	2,700	276
Total time allowed (hours)	—	—	2,258	—	2,441
Time taken (hours clocked)				—	3,446
Labour utilization (Total time allowed for actual workload ÷ time taken × 100)				—	71%

Budget percentage	Budgets			
(To adjust average workload budget to actual workload budget) $\frac{\text{Total time allowed for actual workload } 2{,}441}{\text{Total time allowed for average workload } 2{,}258} \times 100 = 108\%$	Maximum allowed at average workload	Maximum allowed at actual workload	Actual	Difference
Personnel	14	15	21	+6
Controllable expenses	£	£	£	£
Stationery	160	173	205	+32
Telephones	88	95	90	−5
Total	248	268	295	+27
Arrears of work				
No. of lines	172	186	681	495
Total				

Rating	Total	Labour utilization	Expense control	Arrears
Maximum possible points	100	80	10	10
Percentage utilization achieved (Maximum allowed ÷ actual × 100)	—	71%	90%	20%
Points gained	66·0	56·8	9·0	2·0
		Previous month	Average 3 months	
Final rating	66·0	66·5	68·3	—

as readily to other forms of activity. The control statement shown on page 123 applies to a general sales office.

The following points should be noted:

1 The work of the office has been studied in detail and time standards have been developed for the normal operations. The establishment of time standards enables the time allowed for the actual workload to be calculated. The time allowed is compared with the time taken and a measure of labour utilization is calculated.

2 The actual workload is compared with the average workload and this relationship is used to calculate the flexible budget for personnel, controllable expenses, and arrears of work. The actual achievement is compared with the flexible budget, and the difference is shown.

3 The performance of the supervisor is judged according to his control of labour utilization, expense, and arrears of work. A final rating figure is obtained from the weighted average achievement over these three factors.

4 In this example, labour utilization is unsatisfactory and it is possible that some redeployment of personnel may be necessary. Despite overstaffing, arrears of work are much greater than anticipated, and there may be some lack of control in use of stationery. What does the manager do with this control statement? He seeks explanations for the variances and takes action to improve the situation in line with the established standards of performance.

Problem of Accuracy

With the examples of a general machine shop and a general sales office, it has been possible to establish accurate time standards, after a careful examination of the methods of operation. However, it is not always possible to calculate scientific standards. Nevertheless, an essential element in the job of management is to evaluate performance, and this responsibility cannot be shirked. Some predetermined targets must be set, even though they may not be completely accurate. The key factor is to plan and control activities on the basis of a high level of efficiency.

SUMMARY

1 *What is meant by control?*

By control we mean the taking of action in accordance with a pre-determined plan, and the subsequent measurement and evaluation of that action.

2 *What control information does the manager require?*

(a) The manager needs prompt information on the actual level of those costs over which he can exercise a considerable influence.
(b) He also needs a statement showing what these costs should have been.
(c) As further help in the process of evaluation, he needs a statement highlighting and analysing the difference between the actual level of costs and what these costs should have been.

3 *Who is responsible for establishing standards of performance?*

The responsibility for setting standards of performance rests with the individual manager.

4 *What is a standard labour cost?*

A standard labour cost is a pre-determined cost based on an assessment of operations, machines, and type of labour necessary to produce a product efficiently, and the time taken to do so. A rate of pay is related to this.

5 *What is a standard material cost?*

A standard material cost is an estimated cost, based on a technical specification of the materials, making due allowance for reasonable scrap and waste, and priced at the expected price level over a reasonable period.

6 *What is a flexible budget?*

A flexible budget is a budget, usually referring to overhead costs only, which is prepared for a range rather than for a single level of activity. The budget can be automatically geared to changes in the level of volume. Direct labour and direct material are sometimes included in the flexible budget.

CHAPTER 11 | Cost Reduction

In the previous chapter the emphasis was on cost control. We must now turn to the matter of cost reduction. There is a considerable difference between these two techniques. With cost control, we were talking of the guidance and regulation of operating costs by executive action, and the word 'control' implied that some sort of plan was in existence. As explained, this plan might have been expressed in monetary terms in the form of budgets or standards for individual items of cost. Control then involved ensuring that, as far as possible, actual costs were kept in line with the budgets or standards. This is indeed an important task, and is a very considerable challenge for the supervisory manager, but it is not the end of his cost responsibilities. The other responsibility is for cost reduction, which means simply a reduced cost per unit of production. Our aim in cost reduction is to make available the sort of product which the public requires at minimum cost to the producing organization. In other words, in many cases we shall be aiming to reduce the cost of the product without affecting its functions or saleable value. If we have budgets and standards in existence, then cost reduction means challenging these.

Supervisory Responsibilities

In all industrial undertakings management is faced with the task of controlling its operations so that the finished product of the business will be of a specified quality, and produced and sold economically. It is thus essential for everyone in management to accept the responsibility for the output, quality, and cost of the operations in his own division or department of the business. Whatever plan is devised for the control of business operation, the elements of cost must be a vital part of it, and many of these cost elements are incurred in fields where supervisory managers have influence. A supervisory manager should be prepared to look upon the cost responsibility as an opportunity as well as a responsibility. Why is it an opportunity for him? Because he is regarded by a good top management as a key man, in full control of the activities of his department. Top management often judges the supervisory manager's effectiveness on the grounds of cost factors. If he is effective in preventing cost increases and getting cost improvements, then he is bound to be given consideration for promotion and merit increases.

Active participation by a supervisory manager in the work of cost control and cost reduction gives him greater vision and a better insight into managerial duties: it utilizes his ingenuity and increases his job satisfaction. He is in a unique position to observe the factors of cost. A good line supervisor knows his equipment, his personnel, and the products which have to be manufactured. He is on the departmental scene all day and every day, and if he is observant he sees what is going on and hears the reactions of employees. He is in the most favourable position to make assessments of departmental efficiency, and to take the necessary steps to maintain or improve that efficiency.

Cost Reduction and Productivity Improvement

Two factors vitally affect the production costs of an organization, one being the volume of production and the other the efficiency of production. Together, they constitute what is usually called productivity. Let us examine them more closely.

The bigger the volume of output of goods produced or services rendered, the lower will be the unit cost: we have already seen this in examining cost variability. The supervisory manager does have a very considerable responsibility for volume—that is, he is expected to push work through the shop, meet delivery dates, and generally to progress the output. On the other hand, unit costs may also be reduced by greater efficiency, and the supervisory manager is expected to secure achievement of this by the economical use of materials, plant and equipment, space and manpower, together with attention to the important matters of product quality and the incidence of scrap. The link between cost reduction and productivity improvement should now be clear.

Productivity is not easily measured; in fact, there is no agreement in industry about a common measure. In the long term, the best way to measure departmental productivity is to express it in terms of unit cost. By unit cost, we mean the cost of materials, labour, and overhead expenses for each product, or item, or unit of work. It will be an average figure and will include both direct and indirect costs. Assuming stable prices of cost factors, if unit cost rises, then some aspect of departmental productivity is deteriorating. It may be that the total volume of production is decreasing, or that some inefficiency has crept into departmental operations. If unit cost falls, then departmental productivity can be said to have improved, and again this might be due to an improvement in volume or efficiency. It will be seen that we are really measuring productivity in input/output terms. In other words, we are saying that productivity improves when we obtain more output from the same input, or when the input requirement reduces for the same output. In the same way, we are achieving cost reduction when we obtain more output for the same cost, or the same output for less cost.

There is no doubt that top managements of the future will consider the movement of unit costs in a department when evaluating the productivity of the department and the ability of its supervisor. It is therefore necessary for the supervisory manager to pay careful attention to cost factors and measures of productivity.

Purge or Programme? There is no blueprint for cost reduction that can be applied to every organization and every situation, but it has been proved that a systematic approach to the problem helps. After all, what is the alternative to a systematic approach? It is to have occasional drives on particular cost items and purges, but experience shows that these usually dwindle to nothing after a short while: in fact, this method has often produced very harmful results. The purge approach has usually followed one of two patterns:

1 The instruction from somewhere in top management that a 5% across-the-board cost reduction must be achieved. This is unrealistic and an impossibility. There is slack to be taken up in most organizations, but not at the same rate in each department.
2 The attack on one cost in isolation. Successful though this attack might appear to have been, the implications of it are often felt later in other items of cost.

To illustrate the shortcomings of the purge approach, consider the case where an attack is made upon indirect labour costs in a production department and there is a near-indiscriminate slashing of the indirect labour force, with a calculable cost saving. A few days after the event it becomes apparent that the reduction in the indirect labour force has caused productive operators to spend more time in carrying out labouring activities. The result is lower productivity in total, and a higher unit cost in total. It is so easy to make the mistake of concentrating on one cost in one situation, and to ignore the effect on another item of cost, maybe in another situation. The foundry, for example, supplies the machine shop with its castings. There can be some very difficult decisions to make about the wall thicknesses of castings which are to be machined, bearing in mind the costs and facilities of both departments.

When we talk of cost reduction in this book, we are not talking of arbitrary penny-pinching, but of a programmed approach to cost reduction, of a continuous type, and taking into account the broad framework of cost structure. Incidentally, if the last point is to be clearly observed, then a pre-requisite is that we should know our costs. Knowing our costs means knowing the types of expense and also the significance of each type. It means knowing the location of expenditure and the significance of the amount in each location. It is staggering to visit organizations where material is say 65% of total cost, while direct labour is only 8% of total cost, and to find that all the work study effort of recent years has been on the direct labour front. Not that the work study department will have studied direct labour costs alone: it will have studied the productivity of labour in general. But it will not escape the analyst that a $12\frac{1}{2}$% saving on direct labour cost is only equivalent to a $1\frac{1}{2}$% saving in material cost. It might be reasonable to ask the question—has material cost ever been challenged?

There is a role for the supervisory manager in developing a systematic, programmed approach to cost reduction, as will now be demonstrated.

Cost Reduction and Cost Control

Some reiteration is necessary here. First, cost control is aimed at maintaining costs in accordance with established standards. In cost reduction, we must challenge all standards, and endeavour to reduce costs continuously. After all, what has been achieved by controlling costs to existing standards, if the standards contain inefficiencies, and are uncompetitive? In a system of cost control, standards are targets, whereas the cost reduction tries to improve standards. In cost reduction, emphasis is on the present situation and on the future, whereas the normal techniques of cost control are slanted towards the present only. In many organizations these techniques are fairly historical. Cost reduction needs to be applied to all items in every section of the business, whereas cost control is often limited to items which are easily measurable and have standards. Orthodox routines of cost control seek to attain the lowest possible cost per unit under existing conditions. Cost reduction recognizes no condition as permanent, particularly if a change will result in a lower cost.

As a supervisory manager you should know what your costs

are, and how significant each item is. What are the various things which can go wrong in the department and affect costs and productivity? Here are some suggestions.

Production planning
Are *delays* and *holdups* lowering production?
Are *materials ready for use* when received by the worker?
Are operations properly *co-ordinated?*
Are you *planning* operations in advance?

Materials
Are *proper* materials being used?
Are they *uniform* and of *standard* quality?
Are materials *available* when needed?
Are materials and equipment being *properly protected* when not in use?
Are we using the most *economical* material?
Are we using the proper *amount* of material?
Is *standardization* possible?
Can we *start* runs *with scrap?*

Equipment
Is equipment in *satisfactory condition* and properly maintained?
Is equipment the *proper size* for the job?
Is equipment being operated at *optimum speed*, and being properly used at all times?

Layout
Are equipment and materials in work area *arranged* for peak efficiency?
Is the physical *location, size*, and *shape* of work area appropriate?
Are there *distractions* or *inadequacies* that can be corrected?

Procedures
Are procedures in use the most adequate for the job?
Is *unnecessary* time being spent in *make-ready* and *put-away* procedure?
Do waste motions increase time of routine operations?
Are *quality levels* consistent with *requirements?*

Employee training
Are *clear* and *complete* instructions given to employees?
Is guidance offered to new employees or transferred employees?
Are workers encouraged to assist each other in instructions and information?
Is *refresher training* provided to workers when necessary?

Morale

Is there a general *feeling* among the workers that production is adequate and *no improvement* is *necessary?*

Are the factors causing *low morale* also resulting in low output?

Are you using the *right person* for the right job?

Have you considered steps to *improve overall morale?*

Employee abilities

Do your workers possess the *experience necessary* for the job?

Have your workers had *adequate training* for the job?

Are job *requirements too high* for your workers?

Are workers *losing skills?*

Are you *using* all of the workers *skills* in the most efficient manner?

Cost consciousness

Are employees *cost conscious?*

Waste

Can supplies be *reworked* for *reuse?*

Can waste material be made into *by-products* for use or sale?

This is not a complete list—why not make up your own? It will almost certainly be much longer than this one, in which case you have plenty to go at on the cost reduction front. What is now the action required? Well, you might start by gathering the facts that are relevant to answer the questions, or just a few of them to start off with. For instance, in respect of materials, you might:

1 Make an itemized *list* of materials and supplies used.
2 Outline in detail how *'high-cost' materials are being used.*
3 Spot *causes* of extravagant use and look for ways to *eliminate* them.

This will give you some idea of how a cost reduction programme might be initiated.

Scope of Cost Reduction

In practice, cost reduction can only be achieved by regular and repeated action on many fronts, some of which are within the scope of the supervisory manager, others of which are not. If we now look at the whole field of cost reduction, where should our examination start? Logically, it should start at the design stage. It is not always appreciated that the designer holds the initial key to product cost, and operating costs. Every line or squiggle on a drawing gives rise to a cost, and sometimes the lines and squiggles are not too well thought out from the point of view of efficiency and economy in production. Too often, one suspects that the designer is thinking only of the customer, who is indeed an important person, but one who would presumably like to buy at a lower price if redesign would still permit the same finish and functions, and at the same time make for more economical production. Designs and specifications can and should be challenged; the technique of value analysis is useful to this end.

Directly affecting the supervisory manager are the areas of factory layout, plant and equipment, tooling, and production planning, because he has to live in some cases with a poor layout, run-down plant, inadequate tooling, and a lack of production planning. These are all areas to be challenged. If inadequacy in any area gives rise to excessive costs, then it behoves any person in management, no matter at what level, to make sure that this is brought to the attention of those persons who can provide the corrective action required. Indeed, in many cases, the action needed can be recommended or even implemented by the supervisory manager himself.

The area of material cost is a considerable one in most organizations, and to this item there are several possible points of cost reduction. After one has considered the material content specified by design, there is still scope for challenging purchasing, storage, and handling, which may not be directly under the supervisory manager's influence, and then the areas of usage and salvage, which may well be under his direct influence.

How about labour costs, both direct and indirect? A proper examination of this item will entail a look at the process of specifying labour requirements, recruitment, selection and training, as well as observation of the efficiency of the labour force and its deployment. Much can be done by a supervisory manager in regard to these matters, often because of lack of attention to them by others in the management structure.

Why should a supervisory manager be expected to put up with labour with inadequate abilities? He will often be able to improve training facilities and routines.

Again, does he have to live with a method of wage payment which is inadequate and inappropriate to the methods of production? If so, he will not normally be precluded from saying so and from making suggestions to improve the situation.

We must not overlook the importance of volume of production in the matter of unit cost, and the attention which is, therefore, necessary to such matters as down-time and use of facilities generally. Tied up with this will always be the efficiency of production plans and programme, also the adequacy and timetabling of maintenance arrangements.

Use of resources involves the capital employed in the business and, as was made clear earlier on in this book, even this capital has a cost. So it is always worth while challenging what appear to be our capital requirements to see whether any of these could be avoided. If they could, then a cost saving is possible. This leads us to the point that every decision on the use of capital needs to be challenged also, for instance when we are deciding whether or not to purchase a new piece of plant or equipment.

The installation of cost reduction programmes frequently reveals that a very large part of the cost reduction which is possible arises because of inadequate evaluation and poor decision making in the first instance.

In most organizations of any size, the supervisory manager has around him certain specialists who can help him considerably with the work of cost reduction. The work study engineer, for example, is in a unique position to assist on layout, methods, setting targets, and applying correct methods of remuneration. The production controller can help in planning the work of the department and rerouting as necessary. Large modern businesses have specialists in network analysis and critical path evaluation, both of which have their place in cost reduction and profit improvement. Quality control can be improved by statisticians.

The presence of specialists, however, should not blind us to the everyday work of cost reduction which can be practised by any supervisory manager. The presence of a work study expert, for example, does not stop the supervisory manager from implementing his own ideas for work simplification and for reduction of motions and travel. Specialists in an organization are there to be called upon by line management when their expert services are required.

SUMMARY

1 *What is implied by cost reduction, and how does it differ from cost control?*

Cost reduction is aimed at reducing the cost of the product without affecting its functions or saleable value, whereas cost control implies keeping costs within pre-determined budgets or standards. Cost reduction implies a challenging of existing standards.

2 *Why is cost reduction an opportunity for the supervisory manager?*

Because the supervisory manager is regarded by top management as a key man and is judged, amongst other things, on cost factors. Apart from this, cost reduction utilizes the ingenuity of the supervisor and increases his job satisfaction.

3 *Do cost reduction and productivity improvement go hand-in-hand?*

Yes. An improvement in. productivity will lead to a reduction in unit cost. Indeed, the best way to measure productivity is in unit cost terms.

4 *How should one approach the job of cost reduction?*

There is no blueprint for cost reduction but a systematic approach helps. The alternative to a systematic approach is the purge, but experience shows that this method tends to have an effect which dwindles to nothing and often produces harmful results.

5 *How should the supervisory manager in particular make out a cost reduction programme?*

First, he should ask himself what are the various things that can go wrong in the department which may have an effect upon costs and productivity. This can be done under the main headings of Materials, Equipment, Layout, Procedures, etc. Next, he needs to establish what action is required, and then take it. Lastly the results of the action should be evaluated.

6 *How large is the scope of cost reduction?*

Very large. In practice, cost reduction can only be achieved by regular and repeated action on many fronts, some of which are within the scope of the supervisory manager. The cost reduction field extends from decisions on product design to the procedures for despatch, with a big area in between.

7 *What do we mean when we say that costs are the result of decisions?*

All the costs incurred in a business should be incurred consciously—in other words, decisions should have been made which took into account the cost factors. So often, excess costs are the result of faulty decisions.

In previous chapters we have been examining the problems of the individual firm in attempting to secure the most effective use of all available resources. The State, as the largest organization in the country, must also deal with this problem of managing the economy. We have defined planning as an essential factor in the job of any supervisory manager, and this responsibility must also be taken up by the State. Nowadays all political parties agree that a certain amount of State planning is necessary, but there is disagreement as to the extent of the direction which should be exercised by the State. At one extreme there is the State which gears planning to consumer demand, and allows the price mechanism to distribute resources. At the other extreme there is the State, committed to maximum planning, which emphasizes the function of production in relationship to the total plan rather than in satisfaction of consumer demand. Between these two extremes is the middle way taken by Great Britain, which leads to a mixed economy consisting of a private sector, pursuing private enterprise, and a public sector, involving centralized State planning and control.

Objectives of State Planning
The objectives of State planning in Great Britain are fourfold:

1 To maintain a high and stable level of employment.
2 To stabilize the internal purchasing power of money.
3 To obtain steady economic growth and improvement in the standard of living.
4 To protect the nation's balance of payments.

There is no disagreement as to the desirability in principle of these four objectives, but the relative emphasis to be placed on each of them is debated.

State Planning Controls
The methods by which the objectives of State planning are pursued involves three types of control:

1 *Fiscal controls.* These are included in the budgeting procedure of the Government.
2 *Monetary controls.* These are intended to affect the supply and

135

demand for money and credit, and also to influence the
balance of the country's external assets and liabilities.

3 *Physical controls*. These are designed to influence the use and
deployment of physical resources.

Fiscal and Monetary Controls

We can visualize the mixed economy of Great Britain as being
like two large tanks, one representing the public sector and the other
the private sector. The two tanks are linked by pipes; the water in
the pipes represents the monetary system. The Government is
responsible for the level of water in each tank, and also for the rate
of flow in the system.

We should add that our national tanks must be connected to
other national tanks, which will also involve inflows and outflows of
finance.

The Government can affect the level of water in the tanks by
its planning in the Budget. In pre-war years official opinion held
that very little additional employment and no permanent additional
employment could, as a general rule, be created by State borrowing
and State expenditure. This view was confounded by the teachings of
Lord Keynes in his book *The General Theory of Employment,
Interest and Money*. Since the war the management of the National
Debt has become an integral and indispensable part of the British
financial system. State borrowing is of three main kinds:

Long-term borrowing on the stock market by the issue of
Government securities.
Short-term borrowing by issuing Treasury Bills of Exchange.
National Savings of various kinds.

The management of the National Debt, together with the
planning of the level of Government income and expenditure,
represents a major element in the control of the economy. The level
of Government income is geared to the level of taxation, both
direct and indirect. Government expenditure covers both current
expenses and capital expenditure. In total, Government income must
equal Government expenditure, but the importance of the National
Debt is that it can be used as a balancing factor.

The Government can also affect the level of demand and
employment by controlling the supply of money and credit. The
controls in this field are mainly through the joint stock banks and
through hire purchase companies.

The Chancellor of the Exchequer, through the Bank of England, gives official guidance to the joint stock banks about the volume and type of lending to customers. In addition the banks are required from time to time to make special deposits to the Bank of England, which has the effect of reducing the volume of bank lending which is commercially practicable.

The control of hire purchase finance is administered by the Board of Trade, mainly through the terms offered to customers. The control covers the minimum down payment and the maximum periods of repayment.

The State also plans to achieve its objectives by manipulating interest rates. The main weapon is the bank rate, which is the minimum official rate at which the Bank of England will lend money on short-term by taking over Treasury Bills and other first-class bills. The attempt is to alter the short-term rates of interest and, through these, the long-term rate of interest. The main effect of this weapon lies in its influence upon financial opinion both in this country and abroad as to the future intentions of the Government.

The price-wage inflationary spiral has been a persistent problem in State planning since the war. The Government can expect to influence the pricing policies of nationalized industries, but its influence on prices in the private sector rests mainly on the effects of fiscal and monetary measures. Prices, however, affect the cost of living, and therefore become an influence in wage demands. In addition, employers have competed against each other for scarce labour and as a result earnings of workers have often been greatly in excess of nationally agreed standard rates. The requirement is, therefore, a prices and incomes policy. However, the difficulty is how to administer such a policy in a free mixed economy.

Physical Controls
The most important physical controls used in State planning since 1945 have been:

1 Control of production and the distribution of scarce raw materials.
2 Import and export licensing.
3 Building licensing.
4 Control of the location of industry.

The first three controls were relaxed by the early 1950s but the control of the location of industry is important to the individual firm at the present time.

Location of industry. There are two main problems here:

1 Obtaining a balanced distribution of industry and population over the whole country.
2 Unemployment in specific areas.

The controls used to deal with these problems have attempted:

1 To keep industry out of Greater London, Greater Birmingham, and other areas where unemployment has been low.
2 To take work to areas where unemployment has been high.

There are a number of advantages accruing to an industry when it is concentrated in one area:

1 Individual firms can specialize in single processes, or in special varieties of a commodity.
2 Subsidiary industries can develop to service the needs of the major industries.
3 Highly organized markets can develop to deal in the products of the industry.

In view of these advantages, an individual firm might well be attracted to a highly concentrated area by the prospect of low operating costs.

There is, however, a serious disadvantage of the localization of industry. If a district is dependent upon a single basic industry, a change in demand may result in structural unemployment. Areas of localized industries are liable to more severe unemployment than areas with more diversified industries. This was the experience in the 1930s if we compare the unemployment figures of Jarrow and Merthyr with those of Middlesex and Birmingham.

To overcome the disadvantages of the localization of industry, and as a part of the policy to maintain full employment, the Government must exercise some control over the location of industry.

In Great Britain, certain areas are designated development districts and there are various inducements for firms to site their establishments in those areas rather than elsewhere. The Board of Trade may build trading estates, and the Treasury may make grants or loans to firms. Tax advantages are also available.

The Town and Country Planning Act and the New Towns Act

also represent attempts to plan the location of industry and population.

On the one hand, as a trading nation we must maintain and improve our competitive position, therefore, the economic advantages of localization should not be underestimated. On the other hand, we cannot afford to ignore the social costs and implications of localization. A flexible plan must take both aspects into account.

State Promotion

In addition to the economic planning which we have now considered the Government also attempts to promote the interests of industry in other ways.

The range of this sponsorship is very wide. It covers the provision of finance through the Industrial and Commercial Finance Corporation and the Finance Corporation of Industry; the promotion of research; the provision of services to increase productivity, efficiency, and exports through such bodies as the British Productivity Council, the British Standards Institution, National Economic Development Councils, and Regional Planning Boards. It includes the encouragement of joint consultation in industry and assistance in the settlement of disputes; the provision of employment services and the support of training schemes. The development of Agricultural Marketing Boards and the Fish Authorities are examples of Government sponsorship in the field of distribution.

The State has also promoted schemes for the reorganization of industry. This has resulted in three main types of reorganization.

1 The reorganization of some basic industries under public ownership. Examples are electricity, gas, railways, and coal.
2 The reorganization of some basic industries without full public ownership. Examples are civil aviation and road transport.
3 Schemes of rationalization, particularly in those industries in which the Government is a very large buyer—for example, aircraft manufacture, telecommunications equipment, and shipbuilding.

State Regulation

We have seen that the State acts as planner and promoter; we must finally consider the State as regulator—that is, when the

Government intervenes to place legal obligations or restrictions on the conduct of industry.

The affairs of companies and to a lesser extent the affairs of trade unions are regulated by specific Acts of Parliament. In addition to the Companies Acts, 1948 and 1967, which deal with the legal responsibilities of individual companies, the Restrictive Trade Practices Act, 1956, is concerned with the regulation of agreements between companies which are in restraint of competition.

While the Government does not in principle regulate the amount of wages paid by employers, intervention is necessary in those trades where bargaining machinery is inadequate. Enforceable minimum wages in these trades are set by wages councils. Each council consists of equal numbers of representatives of employers and employees, together with not more than three independent members. This method of wage fixing applies to 5 million workers.

Further intervention by the State has been necessary to enforce satisfactory minimum standards of conditions of work. This regulation is covered by the Factories Acts, and other Acts specifically concerned with conditions in mining and quarrying, transport, agriculture, shops, and offices.

In short, the Government acts as planner, promoter, and regulator. These activities can have vital effects on the economic life of individual firms, and thus influence the financial aspects of management.

SUMMARY

1 *State the various roles of the State.*

The State can be regarded firstly as a planner, secondly as a promoter, and thirdly as a regulator.

2 *What are the objectives of State planning?*
The objectives are fourfold:

(a) To maintain a high and stable level of full employment.
(b) To stabilize the internal purchasing power of money.
(c) To obtain steady economic growth and improvement in the standard of living.
(d) To protect the nation's balance of payments.

3 *What are the controls used in State planning?*

The controls used are (a) fiscal, (b) monetary, and (c) physical.

(a) *Fiscal controls.* These controls are included in the budgeting procedure of the Government.

(b) *Monetary controls.* These measures are intended to affect the supply and demand for money and credit, and also to influence the balance of the country's external assets and liabilities.

(c) *Physical controls.* These methods are designed to influence the use and deployment of physical resources.

4 *What are the two main problems associated with planning the location of industry?*

The two main problems involved in planning the location of industry are (a) unemployment in specific areas, and (b) obtaining a balanced distribution of industry and population over the whole country.

5 *Mention the ways in which the State acts as promoter.*

The areas of promotion include finance, research, productivity, efficiency, exports, industrial relations, employment services, marketing, and the reconstruction of industry.

6 *Mention the ways in which the State acts as regulator.*

The areas of regulation include the administration of limited liability companies, agreements in restraint of competition, minimum enforceable wages, fixed standards of conditions of work.

Further Reading

Chambers, R. J. *Financial Management*. Sweet & Maxwell, London (1954).

Clemens, J. H. *Balance Sheet and the Lending Banker* (3rd edition). Europa Publications, London (1965).

Edey, H. C. *Business Budgets and Accounts* (3rd edition). Hutchinson, London (1966).

Grove, J. W. *Government and Industry in Britain*. Longmans, London (1962).

Paish, F. W. *Business Finance* (3rd edition). Pitman, London (1965).

Rose, H. B. *The Economic Background to Investment*. Cambridge University Press, London (1960).

Rose, T. G. *Higher Control in Management* (7th edition). Pitman, London (1963).

Solomons, D. (ed.) *Studies in Costing* (2nd edition). Sweet & Maxwell, London (1968).

Accountancy. Institute of Chartered Accountants (monthly).

Management Accounting. Institute of Cost and Management Accountants (monthly).

Index